–PRAISE FOR THIS BOOK–

Mel K reveals the rise of a global elite who infiltrated our country instead of invading it. She exposes the betrayal of Americans by that invisible system of global control whose target is the national sovereignty of every Democratic state. Mel K sets the stage for The Great Reckoning that Americans must demand as a free nation.

—**ROSEANNE BARR**, actress, comedian, writer, producer

With her signature clarity and fearless insight, Mel K delivers a groundbreaking exposé of the silent coup that reshaped America after World War II. While the nation celebrated victory, the Dulles brothers and Rockefeller network quietly orchestrated Operation Paperclip, the Velvet Empire, the Invisible State, and the Red House Legacy—choosing infiltration over invasion to embed a technocratic globalist agenda. With her sharp analysis and powerful storytelling, Mel K reveals how these architects secured a monopoly on power and expertise, birthing today's Deep State and cultural elite. This book is a must-read that only Mel K could write—brilliant, urgent, and impossible to ignore.

—**JIMMY DORE**, comedian, political commentator

Through solid research and remarkable insight, Mel K has written a brilliant exposé of the global shadows of power that have usurped our Constitutional form of government. In impressive detail, Mel K reveals the strategic convergence of foundations, intelligence agencies, banking systems, multinational corporations, and the United Nations that has gained control over our elected government. This is a must-read for every American.

—**KEVIN SHIPP**, former CIA Officer, author of *Twilight of the Shadow Government: How Transparency Will Kill the Deep State*

Mel K's ability to break down the Globalists' complex architecture and their long-standing plans is unmatched, whether on her show or in writing. This book is no exception, and as a passionate researcher of U.S. history, I could not put it down. *Infiltration Instead of Invasion: America Betrayed (1944–1954)* is a must-read to understand the state in which the U.S.A. finds herself today and, hopefully, guide Americans to rectify this grave betrayal. The survival of the Republic depends on it.

—**NOOR BIN LADIN**, political commentator, writer

Infiltration Instead of Invasion is another must-read Mel K masterpiece. History has been strategically altered for generations, underMinding America's Constitutional values of freedom and justice for ALL. Mel K sets the record straight, righting history with concise and comprehensive facts while reminding us how to critically analyze, thoroughly research, and discern truth that makes us free. Whether she is empowering us through her popular podcasts, brilliance onstage, monuMental book *Americans Anonymous*, or is revealing the darkest depths of corruption in her timely book release *Infiltration Instead of Invasion*, Mel K is an abSOULute national treasure to u.s. all. Embrace your right to truth today with Mel K.

—**CATHY O'BRIEN**, author of numerous books, including *Trance Formation of America* and *Access Denied for Reasons of National Security*

The decade following World War II was the most consequential period of history, which largely defined the postwar global order that has defined our political, economic, and social reality to this day. It is also easily the most overlooked part of our history, and a deep, critical account of it was overdue. Mel K rose to the challenge admirably, capturing this critical time in authoritative and beautifully captivating prose. For anyone wishing to understand today's events, this is a must-read! A deep bow to the author.

—**ALEX KRAINER**, market analyst, author, former hedge fund manager

As we come to the end of a Fourth Turning and reflect on where the cycle began, we are reminded of the importance of the decade immediately following World War II. The institutional framework laid during this pivotal period spawned the bloodthirsty American Empire, created the surveillance state, and saw the U.S. Dollar used to club disobedient countries into submission. Mel brilliantly and methodically details this critical decade and connects the dots that help to make sense of today's global events. This book is Mel's magnum opus and an instant classic.

—**CHARLIE ROBINSON**, #1 best-selling author, *The Controlled Demolition of the American Empire,* editor, Activist Post

With this book, Mel K has managed to unravel an abiding mystery of our time—who planted the seeds of rot in the major institutions of American life that have wrecked our politics. It's a tale of arrogant utopianism gone off the rails, turning leadership into America's own worst enemy and setting our republic on fire.

—**JAMES HOWARD KUNSTLER**, author of numerous books, including *The Long Emergency* and *The Geography of Nowhere*

Mel K's *Infiltration Instead of Invasion* is a really smart book with a provocative and original thesis. Yes, America was infiltrated in the post-World War II years, and it was not necessarily by the Alger Hiss and Julius Rosenberg types. Their damage had largely been done by the time the war was over. No, the infiltrators in question were the "industrial magnates, central bankers, and administrators groomed by foundations that spoke the language of global interdependence."

This was not so much a conspiracy as a simple reality. As Americans began to enjoy the stability of the postwar return to normality, they failed to understand the chaos into which the rest of the world had descended. They also failed to see the long-term designs of the global institutions that had readied themselves for just such a moment.

In lesser hands, this book is a conspiratorial polemic with villains on every other page. In Mel K's able hands, this book is an education.
—**JACK CASHILL**, author of numerous books, producer, media consultant

INFILTRATION INSTEAD OF INVASION

AMERICA BETRAYED

(1944–1954)

Mel K

Harvest Creek®

"For we are opposed around the world by a monolithic and ruthless conspiracy that relies primarily on covert means for expanding its sphere of influence—on infiltration instead of invasion, on subversion instead of elections, on intimidation instead of free choice, on guerrillas by night instead of armies by day. It is a system which has conscripted vast human and material resources into the building of a tightly knit, highly efficient machine that combines military, diplomatic, intelligence, economic, scientific, and political operations.

Its preparations are concealed, not published. Its mistakes are buried, not headlined. Its dissenters are silenced, not praised. No expenditure is questioned, no rumor is printed, no secret is revealed."

—President John F. Kennedy
Address to the American Newspaper Publishers Association,
Waldorf-Astoria Hotel, New York City, April 27, 1961

Every effort has been made to ensure that all the information in this book is accurate at the time of publication. If you have questions or comments about this book or need information about special sales or bulk purchases, please contact Harvest Creek Publishing & Design at info@harvestcreek.net.

The views expressed in this book are the author's and do not necessarily reflect those of the publisher.

Library of Congress Control Number: 2026909267

First Edition:
ISBN: 978-1-961641-49-5

Mel K provides resources and content on a wide range of topics, as well as being available for speaking events. Find out more at https://themelkshow.com.

Book Cover & Layout by Harvest Creek Publishing & Design, Conroe, TX

Printed in Canada

–DEDICATION–

This book is dedicated to every American who sensed something was wrong long before they had the words to explain it.

It is for the citizens who still believe freedom is worth the fight.

It is for my father, who taught me to see the unseen and never surrender the truth.

It is for Rob—protective, unwavering, and deeply loved. You held the line when it mattered most. My Hero!

–CONTENTS–

–INTRODUCTION–

> *"The most dangerous untruths are truths moderately distorted."*
>
> GEORG CHRISTOPH LICHTENBERG

THE HISTORY OF A NATION is rarely written in the places we expect it. It does not always unfold in the chambers of Congress, or in the great archives where parchment ages in climate-controlled silence. Sometimes a country's fate turns in the corners of the world least illuminated, in rooms where the minutes are never taken, in conversations that pass between men who possess no mandate from the public yet act with authority greater than any election could bestow. These are the shadows where systems are shaped long before they bear names, where decisions are made that will reverberate across continents and decades, touching lives that will never know the forces acting upon them.

The decade between 1944 and 1954 belongs to that kind of history. It is a period often described as a "transition," a bridge from war to peace, from crisis to prosperity, from the exhaustion of a global catastrophe to the invigorating promise of an American century. But transition is too gentle a word. A bridge is too innocent an image. What happened in those ten years was nothing less than a reconstruction of the modern world—quietly, meticulously undertaken by men who understood that the most consequential revolutions are the ones conducted in silence.

When the war ended, Americans believed they had earned a return to normal life. Soldiers came home and married. The GI Bill opened the doors of universities to a generation that had never imagined itself on a campus. Suburbs spread across open land like declarations of optimism.

Children were born at such a pace that demographers were left scrambling for new language. Victory was not only military; it appeared moral, cultural, and national. The United States seemed to stand not merely atop the world but somehow outside of it, immune to the ancient frictions that kept other nations shackled to their historical contexts.

But beneath the celebration, another story took form—one that existed beyond the visibility of parades and speeches, one written not in headlines but in contracts, alliances, memoranda, and institutional blueprints. It was a story of networks rather than nations, of systems rather than slogans, of continuity rather than rupture. It was the story of how the old world, defeated in battle, found new life in the emerging architecture of global governance, and how the new world, triumphant on every front, found itself adopting the very tools of influence and control it believed it had destroyed.

This book is an excavation of that story. It is an attempt to trace the lines of power that slipped unnoticed into the postwar world, to uncover the blueprints drafted in Basel, Bern, New York, London, Frankfurt, and Washington, to illuminate the quiet ascent of institutions built not to serve citizens but to outlast them.

It is a narrative of decisions made behind closed doors, often justified in the language of necessity, frequently shielded by the rhetoric of peace, and almost always insulated from democratic oversight. Rather than military force, it was accomplished through the embedding of ideas, the management of economies, the shaping of institutions, and the cultivation of elites who would carry forward a vision of world order that answered not to voters but to networks.

The journey begins in Basel, where a bank unlike any other waited out the war with the composure of an institution certain of its own destiny. The Bank for International Settlements (BIS), born in the wreckage of World War I and matured through the chaos of World War II, emerged from the conflict not as a remnant of the old order but as the quiet custodian of the new one. It facilitated transactions that moved through the cracks of wartime morality. It protected relationships that transcended loyalty to any flag. And when the guns fell silent, it was standing, unshaken, untouched, and poised to play a defining role in the reconstruction of Europe and the globalization of financial governance.

From there, the narrative follows the men who shaped the postwar decade—not the elected leaders whose portraits adorn history books, but the architects who operated beneath them. The Dulles brothers, trained in the crucible of Wall Street internationalism, understood the power of treaties, alliances, and covert operations long before those tools became normalized instruments of statecraft. They saw the world not as a collection of sovereign nations but as a network of interests that must be harmonized toward stability. Stability, however, carried a meaning they rarely articulated directly: The preservation of systems that placed decision-making in the hands of those who understood how the machinery worked.

Rockefeller foundations and affiliated institutions took on roles that blurred the boundary between philanthropy and policy, shaping the intellectual landscape of the postwar world, training the next generation of global administrators, and funding projects that nudged nations toward international integration. Universities, think tanks, research councils, and cultural organizations became conduits of ideology, not conspiracy, but worldview. A worldview that believed governance should rise above borders, that sovereignty should bend to interdependence, and that democracy, while noble, required guidance from those capable of mastering complexity.

Operation Paperclip entered this architecture with the force of a moral paradox: A program that embraced the scientific genius of the defeated regime while sanitizing its crimes for strategic gain. The German scientists who arrived in America brought with them not only their expertise but their assumptions about hierarchy, secrecy, technocracy, and the use of science as an instrument of state power. They influenced aerospace, intelligence, medicine, education, and psychology in ways that would expand far beyond the laboratories where they began. The very institutions that claimed to defend democracy found themselves reshaped by a talent pool drawn from one of history's most anti-democratic regimes.

Meanwhile, the United Nations, celebrated as a symbol of global cooperation, quietly became something more structural. Its agencies developed immunities and mandates that allowed them to function above national law. In theory, they existed to prevent war and promote peace. In practice, they laid the groundwork for a system of governance in which authority migrated upward, away from citizens and toward institutions that saw themselves as the custodians of global norms. These institutions were guided by experts, not elected representatives, by administrators, not assemblies. Their power resided not in force but in the slow accretion of jurisdiction over health, education, labor, agriculture, finance, children's welfare, and human rights—domains once held firmly within the purview of sovereign states.

All these streams converged into what this book calls "The Velvet Empire," a structure of power that expanded its reach not through conquest but through interdependence. Its strength lay not in visibility but in invisibility, not in declarations but in agreements, not in armies but in networks. By 1954, the architecture was in place. When the scaffolding was removed, what remained was a system capable of guiding nations without being elected by them. It was a system that could endure changes in administration, ideology, or public opinion because its authority did not originate from the public in the first place.

And yet, for decades, most citizens sensed none of this. Life improved. Opportunities expanded. Technology advanced with breathtaking speed.

The Cold War provided a narrative that framed the postwar order as a bulwark against tyranny. America prospered, and with prosperity came trust—a trust that allowed the invisible system to deepen its roots without challenge.

But history tends to reveal itself when the consequences of past decisions can no longer be concealed within the language of necessity. The warnings that President John F. Kennedy delivered in 1961 about a "monolithic and ruthless conspiracy that relies … on infiltration instead of invasion, on subversion instead of elections" echoed not only the threats posed by foreign adversaries but the quiet realities of a world already shaped by institutions operating beneath the thresholds of public awareness. And the caution offered by George Washington in his Farewell Address—that the nation must guard against entangling alliances and the concentration of power—resonated with a clarity that hindsight sharpens into revelation.

This book is not an indictment. It is a revelation. It does not claim that the men who shaped the postwar world set out to undermine the republic. Many believed they were saving it, protecting it from the dangers of extremism, nationalism, and global instability. But intentions do not erase outcomes. The systems built between 1944 and 1954 reshaped the American republic in ways few citizens understood. Sovereignty became porous. Decision-making migrated upward and outward. Our democratic republic became entangled with institutions whose interests were not always aligned with those of the people.

What follows is the story of that transformation.

This is the puzzle that asks the "How" questions. How national independence gave way to global interdependence. How wartime alliances became permanent architectures. How financial institutions gained jurisdiction over policy. How intelligence agencies evolved into instruments of influence beyond their mandates. How the rhetoric of unity concealed the reality of consolidation, and finally, how patient, systematic infiltration replaced invasion as the method by which the modern world was reordered.

This is not conspiracy theory. This is documentary history. Drawn from declassified archives, diplomatic correspondence, economic records, intelligence histories, and the work of scholars who spent their lives tracing the contours of hidden power, this book reconstructs a decade that refuses to recede into the past. It reveals how the events of those years influenced the world we inhabit today, and how the choices made by men long gone continue to determine the boundaries of sovereignty, the limits of democracy, and the trajectory of a nation founded on the radical idea that government derives its legitimacy from the consent of the governed.

Infiltration Instead of Invasion is both a chronicle and an invitation. It invites the reader to follow the clues left behind in archives and footnotes, to see the world not as it was advertised but as it was assembled, and to reclaim the understanding that sovereignty is not a relic but a responsibility. Each generation must renew this covenant if it is to survive.

The decade that followed the war never ended.

Its architecture surrounds us still.

This is the story of how it was built.

–CHAPTER ONE–

BASEL'S GHOST

> *"The process by which banks create money is so simple that the mind is repelled."*
> JOHN KENNETH GALBRAITH

THE RHINE MOVES WITH a kind of ancient patience through Basel, as if the river has long made peace with the fact that empires rise and fall on its banks. Even in the closing years of World War II, when Europe burned from the edges inward, and entire nations seemed to tremble under the weight of their own futures, the river kept its steady rhythm. It slid beneath the bridges and past the spired medieval roofs with a silent indifference, carrying no hint of the secrets held in the modest stone building near the Centralbahnplatz.

Nothing about that building announced the enormity of what transpired inside. It bore no grand columns, no sculpted pediments proclaiming power. A passerby might have mistaken it for an insurance office or a municipal archive. Yet in its unassuming halls, guarded more by discretion than by force, sat the institution that would shape the postwar era more profoundly than most governments: The Bank for International Settlements (BIS).

To grasp what the BIS was in those final years of the war, and what it would become in the decade that followed, one must understand its most elusive quality—its ability to survive. The bank had been born from the rubble of the First World War, designed initially to administer German reparations.

But even as the political structures that created it began to crumble, the BIS evolved, adapted, and endured. It was never a bank in the ordinary sense. It had no allegiance to any country, no electorate to answer to, no democratic process to restrain it. The BIS was a creature of treaties and sovereign immunities, insulated from the jurisdiction of the very nations whose central banks it served.

Its architects believed that finance must stand above the volatility of politics, that the flow of money must remain uninterrupted by the burdens of accountability or public sentiment. And so, the BIS was placed in a realm uniquely its own—protected, extraterritorial, and discreet. It was a sovereign entity nestled inside a sovereign nation, yet answerable to neither.

By 1944, as Allied forces fought toward the heart of the Reich and the end of the war became an ever-closer certainty, the BIS functioned like the still eye of a storm. Outside its walls, the continent was racked by violence, hunger, occupation, and uncertainty. Inside, the bank's governors convened with the solemn composure of men conducting business in peacetime.

The Swiss clocks in its corridors ticked with regulatory precision. Files were arranged neatly in metal cabinets. Telegraphs clicked with understated authority. The calmness was not a veneer but a statement—a declaration that the world of high finance answered to a rhythm older and more enduring than the rise and fall of nations.

Thomas McKittrick, the American who presided over the BIS during the war, embodied the paradox of the institution. To Washington, he was a private banker on temporary leave. To Basel, he was the custodian of continuity. To Germany, he was a useful intermediary. And to history, he became the figure at the center of one of the most morally ambiguous chapters in the story of global governance.

Thomas Harrington McKittrick was born in St. Louis in 1889, the son of a dry-goods merchant. He attended Harvard, joined Lee, Higginson & Company—one of Boston's most prominent banking houses—and built a transatlantic career as a bond specialist through the 1920s and 1930s. By the time he arrived in Basel in 1940 to assume the presidency of the Bank for International Settlements, he was fifty years old, silver-haired, and fluent in five languages. To the men who worked beside him, he appeared the ideal choice: Polished enough for European banking society, American enough to reassure Washington, and discreet enough to manage an institution whose wartime conduct would later require all the discretion he possessed.

From his corner office on the third floor of the BIS building near the Centralbahnplatz, McKittrick presided over something that had no name in any legal framework and no precedent in any history of warfare: An active financial institution whose board included representatives of nations currently at war with one another. The German director, Emil Puhl, was vice president of the Reichsbank. The Italian director represented the Bank of Italy. The Japanese director served Tokyo. McKittrick chaired meetings at which these men sat alongside their British and French counterparts—men whose governments were killing one another on a continental scale. There, they discussed monetary settlements with the calm professionalism of insurance actuaries.

He justified this with a consistency that impressed even his critics. The global financial system was a mechanism, he argued, not a moral actor. Its function was to process and clear. If it stopped functioning during wartime, the damage to every postwar economy—Allied and Axis alike—would be incalculable. McKittrick believed this. His correspondence with the Federal Reserve Bank of New York, some of which survived declassification in the 1990s, reveals a man not indifferent to the war's moral dimensions but genuinely convinced that his institution's neutrality served the long-term interests of civilization. He was not cynical. He was certain.

That certainty cost him nothing personally. When investigators from the U.S. Treasury Department and the British Board of Trade examined the BIS's wartime accounts after 1945, they documented gold transfers from the Reichsbank to the BIS valued at approximately 3.7 million Swiss francs at wartime rates—gold that subsequent investigations established included metal looted from occupied central banks and, in at least some portion, from the victims of the regime itself. McKittrick had signed off on these transactions. He had not, in his own account, asked where the gold came from. That question, he suggested, was not his to ask.

He left Basel in 1946, returned to New York, and joined Chase National Bank as a vice president—the same institution that David Rockefeller would later chair, and that would become one of the central nodes in the postwar financial architecture. His career ended without censure, without investigation, without public accounting. The U.S. Treasury's report on the BIS, completed in 1945, recommended the institution's dissolution. That recommendation was shelved.

McKittrick maintained cordial relations with the Reichsbank throughout the war. He corresponded with German industrialists whose factories relied on forced labor. He facilitated transactions that allowed German assets to be repositioned even as Allied troops closed in. McKittrick died in 1970. The BIS continued.

He had been right about one thing. The structural machinery of liquidity survived. The resources moved efficiently and stealthfully. However, he purposely chose not to inquire about the origin of the assets used, nor how they were ultimately dispersed.

All of this he justified with convictions that would become the hallmark of his era:

- The global financial system must be preserved at all costs.
- Economic collapse was more dangerous than moral compromise.
- The machinery of international banking must transcend the messiness of human conflict.

Inside the Bank for International Settlements conference rooms, these justifications were rarely spoken aloud. They did not need to be. The institution drew to itself men who shared an unarticulated code: That money had its own logic, that stability outweighed sentiment, and that certain decisions belonged in rooms without windows.

It was in one such room that the bank's governors, representing nations at war with one another, continued meeting throughout the conflict. British officials sat across from Germans even as their countries exchanged bombs. French representatives attended meetings after their government had fallen. The lines that divided Europe on the battlefield did not divide it here. The BIS had become a sanctuary for a certain kind of power—the power that does not depend on armies, does not answer to elections, and survives occupation, liberation, and regime change with equal indifference.

By the end of the war, the bank's vaults held gold linked to Nazi plunder, much of it transferred through channels deliberately obscured from public view. Committees formed in the United States and the United Kingdom to investigate the BIS's wartime role, and calls were made to dissolve the institution for collaborating with the enemy. But these efforts faltered against a quiet, formidable resistance mounted by the very elites who were preparing to shape the postwar order.

Some argued, persuasively, forcefully, and behind closed doors, that the BIS was too important to dismantle. Europe's recovery would require a stable financial nerve center. The integration of central bank policy would demand a neutral venue. The architects of Bretton Woods, even those troubled by the bank's wartime conduct, acknowledged privately that the BIS was the only institution capable of coordinating the monetary reconstruction of Europe. And so the bank survived, as it had survived every upheaval before.

But survival alone does not explain its significance. What made the BIS central to the emerging global system was not merely its continuity, but the kind of continuity it embodied. It represented a world in which financial interdependence superseded democratic accountability, in which central banks operated with a degree of autonomy that placed them outside the reach of their own governments, and in which decisions made in Basel would shape the economic fates of millions who had never heard of the institution, let alone consented to its authority.

Europe's recovery would require a stable financial nerve center.

Even in 1944, as bombs still fell and regimes still fought for their lives, the BIS was preparing for the next era. It served as the discreet clearinghouse for the reorganization of German industry. This effort aligned with the plans drafted in Strasbourg's Red House, where industrialists and SS intermediaries envisioned a postwar future in which the economic backbone of the Reich would survive under new corporate forms.

It provided a venue where old relationships could be preserved under the guise of necessity. It offered a space where the emerging American financial empire could interface with the remnants of Europe's old order, forging alliances that would shape the Marshall Plan, NATO's economic underpinnings, and the frameworks that eventually evolved into the European Economic Community.

For the men who governed the BIS, the war was not a rupture but a recalibration. The real task was not victory. It was continuity.

In this sense, Basel became a metaphor for the postwar world: A city that outwardly escaped the devastation inflicted upon its neighbors, yet quietly absorbed the shockwaves that rippled across the continent. To walk through its old town in 1944 was to encounter a kind of suspended time. The façades were intact. The shopkeepers carried on. The trams rattled across cobblestones as if nothing had changed. But beneath the veneer lay the reality that the fate of Europe—and eventually of the world—was being reshaped here, in conference rooms where neutrality masked influence and where discretion served as the highest form of power.

Basel's ghost was not the BIS building itself but the philosophy it housed: The belief that global structures must be insulated from the passions of the public, that governance required expertise rather than consent, and that the future should be engineered by those who understood how to balance the ledgers that nations themselves depended upon.

It was a silent belief, spoken rarely, acted upon often, and destined to outlast the century that produced it.

This belief became the thread that wove through the next decade. It was the thread that tied together:

- The reconstruction of Europe
- The integration of international institutions
- The rise of American intelligence networks
- The compromises made in the name of security
- The slow, almost imperceptible shift in the meaning of sovereignty

The story of that transformation begins here, in Basel, where the river kept its ancient rhythm even as the world changed around it, and where the architecture of the modern global order took its first, ghostly shape.

–CHAPTER TWO–

THE RED HOUSE LEGACY

> *"When the war is over, the nation does not recover the money; it is gone, with all the property it once represented."*
>
> WILLIAM GOUGE

THE WAR WAS DYING, though no one in Strasbourg dared say it aloud that August afternoon in 1944. Europe lay in a posture of exhaustion with its armies drained, cities hollowed by bombardment, and entire populations disoriented by the violence that had redrawn the familiar contours of life. The Maison Rouge Hotel, with its polished floors and tired velvet drapes, was one of the few places in the region that still held the illusion of civility. Yet beneath its painted ceilings, on August 10, 1944, a meeting began that had everything to do with the future and almost nothing to do with the collapsing present.

The gathering later came to be known, almost mythically, as the "Red House" meeting. To call it clandestine understates its character. It was a conclave, orchestrated with precision, attended by men who were not accustomed to being directed, yet arrived promptly and without fanfare. They entered through the side entrance, each ushered past the concierge with a nod of recognition from attendants whose discretion had long been paid for. None wore SS uniforms or party insignia. Their power was quieter, older, and more resilient than the symbols of the regime that was disintegrating around them.

They were the industrialists of the Reich—men whose names were not shouted by soldiers but inscribed in ledgers, contracts, and the steel bones of factories. They came from IG Farben, Krupp, Röchling, Thyssen, Siemens, Messerschmitt, Daimler-Benz, pillars of a corporate world that predated Hitler and would survive him. These were the custodians of German industry, the men who had built the machine the regime had ridden into war. They were also the men best positioned to outlive it.

The purpose of the meeting was not ideological. No one discussed the purity of the Aryan race or the future of National Socialism. They discussed survival. Influence. Continuity. What mattered now was not the Reich's fading dream of a thousand-year empire but the preservation of the economic networks that had made Germany formidable long before Hitler arrived. The industrialists knew the war was lost. What they refused to lose was relevance.

An SS liaison opened the meeting by stating, without drama, that Germany must prepare for defeat. The bluntness stunned no one. Intelligence from all fronts pointed toward catastrophe: The Allies were advancing from Normandy, the Soviets from the east, and the Luftwaffe was a shell of its former self. Hitler still raged in his bunkers, but the men gathered in Strasbourg had long ceased to measure the world through his eyes. The Reich might be collapsing, but German industry had the potential to transcend the fall—if it acted quickly.

War destroys nations. But it also rearranges them.

The minutes of this meeting, captured later in U.S. intelligence reports, read less like the remnants of a dying regime and more like the board directives of a multinational conglomerate preparing for restructuring. The industrialists were instructed to cultivate foreign subsidiaries, especially in neutral countries, and to transfer assets into names that would not attract Allied suspicion. They were told to move capital out of Germany quietly, rapidly, and invisibly. The process would be done to store patents abroad and to ensure that technical knowledge, research, and managerial expertise did not vanish with the ruins of Berlin.

War destroys nations. But it also rearranges them.

At the Red House, this simple truth became a strategy. What the SS liaison revealed did not surprise the executives in the room, because many had already begun executing portions of this plan. German industry had always been international in its sensibilities. IG Farben had maintained deep partnerships with American chemical companies—DuPont, Standard Oil—long before the war.

Krupp had business relationships that spanned continents. And Siemens had built telecommunication systems in dozens of countries. These were not provincial enterprises. They were global organisms, adept at adaptation, accustomed to working with whichever governments allowed them to grow.

But now the stakes were existential. The liaison delivered a directive that would become the core of the Red House legacy:

> **The Third Reich would lose the war, but German industrial power must not lose the peace.**

The plan was astonishingly detailed. Assets were to be transferred through Swiss banks, converted into foreign currency, or lodged in shell companies across Portugal, Spain, Sweden, and Latin America. Technical managers were to relocate temporarily, preserving expertise. Factories in Germany would be allowed to fall or be seized by the Allies if necessary; what mattered was the intellectual property, the patents, the network of relationships, and the financial arteries that could be reconnected after the storm passed.

In one particularly telling moment recorded in the Red House documents, an industrialist reportedly remarked that "Nazism will pass, but industry remains." To these men, ideology was a tide. Industry was a continent. They did not speak of Hitler's fate, nor of the atrocities that were by then undeniable to those with access to internal reports. Their concerns were managerial and structural. They saw themselves as stewards of a German destiny larger than any regime—custodians of knowledge, capital, and influence that must be sheltered from Allied retribution if Germany were to rise again. And rise it would.

One of the most disturbing and revealing aspects of the Red House plan was its global scope. Argentina played a key role, particularly under Juan Perón, whose government welcomed German capital, engineers, technicians, and officials with open arms. Networks of exfiltration—ratlines—would later bring not only war criminals but corporate assets into South America. In Brazil, Chile, Uruguay, and Paraguay, German firms established footholds that would become integral to their postwar revival.

But South America was only one prong. The more silent prong moved through Switzerland.

Swiss neutrality was not a moral stance; it was a business model. Throughout the war, Swiss banks had accepted gold, foreign currency, and negotiable instruments from the Reich, including some linked to the plunder of occupied nations. The infrastructure for asset transfer already existed. The Red House meeting merely accelerated what was already in motion: A flurry of financial activity that placed enormous wealth beyond the reach of the Allied occupation authorities.

The BIS in Basel played its own muted role. Its president, Thomas McKittrick, maintained cordial relations with both Allied and Axis central bankers throughout the war. Transactions that moved through the BIS carried the protection of sovereign immunity. The Red House industrialists understood this. Money that passed through Basel could not easily be seized.

When the war ended, Allied investigators found themselves confronting a puzzle with too many missing pieces. They located accounts in Swiss banks that had mushroomed in 1944. They traced corporate transactions that shifted patents into obscure subsidiaries overnight. They uncovered letters hinting at contingency plans. But the webs were too intricate, too skillfully spun, and too protected by the legal armor of neutrality.

The Americans and British, faced with the reality of a looming Cold War, made a decision that proved decisive for the Red House legacy:

> **They stopped asking the questions that would complicate their reconstruction strategy.**

A stable, industrially capable Germany was essential to countering Soviet influence. Purging its economic class would be destabilizing. Bringing its scientific and technical minds to justice would be counterproductive. The logic was brutal in its efficiency. The war was moral; the peace must be strategic.

Thus, the men who sat at the Red House table discovered that their gamble had paid off. When West Germany began its rapid reconstruction, the same industrial titans—not all, but many—returned to positions of influence. IG Farben, formally dissolved by the Allies, reemerged as three successor companies—BASF, Bayer, and Hoechst—each reclaiming portions of the old empire. Krupp reconstituted itself with startling speed. Siemens retooled and expanded. Thyssen merged, maneuvered, and grew. Volkswagen—born from a Nazi vision—became a global brand of democratic prosperity.

To a casual observer, it looked like a miracle—the Wirtschaftswunder, the German economic miracle. But miracles rarely survive close inspection.

What emerged was not a resurrection but a continuation. Germany had not risen from the ashes; the ashes had been swept aside to reveal structures left intact by design.

The significance of the Red House Papers lies in what they reveal about modern power:

The most enduring influence does not reside in armies or governments, but in networks of capital, expertise, and institutional continuity.

This truth would become a defining theme of the coming decade—from the reconstruction of Europe to the rise of multinational corporations. And from the formation of intelligence alliances to the creation of supranational institutions.

The Red House legacy was not a historical footnote. It was the overture to a new world. And its architecture, crafted in a moment of defeat, would become one of the cornerstones of the postwar order—merging seamlessly with American strategic goals, European integration, and the global financial networks centered in Basel.

Yet the true measure of the Red House plan's audacity is not found in the movements of capital or the preservation of patents, but in the muted reconstitution of relationships that would become the connective tissue of the new world emerging from the rubble.

In the immediate aftermath of Germany's surrender, the Allied Control Council attempted, at least initially, to impose a program of denazification that extended into the economic sphere. The idea was straightforward: Dismantle the cartels that had fueled the war machine, strip the industrial elite of its authority, and reorient the German economy toward a democratic ethos.

But the architects of the Red House understood something the Allies were only beginning to learn:

Dismantling a system on paper does not dismantle the men who built it.

When interrogators confronted German industrialists, they discovered a class of executives who had already begun reframing their wartime activities in the language of necessity. They painted themselves not as ideologues but as technocrats. Not as Nazis, but as businessmen navigating a regime they could not resist. Many of them proved startlingly adept at presenting themselves as the only individuals capable of steering Germany toward stability, productivity, and cooperation.

The Allied interrogators, often young officers with limited corporate or financial experience, found themselves outmatched by executives who had spent their lives negotiating across borders and crises. These men spoke with an authority born not of arrogance but of expertise—decades of technical mastery, managerial command, and global relationships that stretched from Buenos Aires to Amsterdam.

To the interrogators, they appeared indispensable. To the industrialists, the moment was merely a negotiation.

The Americans, in particular, began shifting their priorities as the geopolitical landscape clarified. By late 1945, it was unmistakable. The Soviet Union was not simply a wartime ally, but the central challenge of the century.

The task of reconstruction could no longer be divided neatly into moral and practical categories. If Europe were to be shielded from Soviet influence, West Germany would need a functioning industrial base, and rapidly. Washington's strategic pivot opened the door through which the Red House industrialists stepped, not as fugitives from justice but as partners in rebuilding.

The Reich had fallen. Their networks had not.

Even more striking was the discreet involvement of American and British corporate actors, many of whom had maintained business relationships with German firms before the war. Sullivan & Cromwell, the law firm where John Foster Dulles had shaped prewar transatlantic agreements, became an unofficial guide for American companies seeking to navigate the complexities of postwar Germany. The

Rockefeller empire, extending through its foundations and corporate holdings, saw in Germany not a defeated nation but a future anchor of European stability.

The convergence of German industrial survival, Anglo-American strategic necessity, and the early pressures of the Cold War produced a remarkable phenomenon: A postwar Germany rebuilt by many of the same men who had prepared for defeat months before the war's end.

It is impossible to understand this continuity without examining the broader currents of the time. The decade from 1944 to 1954 was not simply a period of reconstruction; it was a period of reorganization. The old world had been shattered, but not all of its components were destroyed. Many were simply rearranged and reassembled into a new configuration that preserved influence while discarding ideology.

The Red House legacy was one of these components.

Consider the case of IG Farben, the chemical conglomerate whose reach extended into pharmaceuticals, synthetic materials, explosives, and fuel. Officially dismantled by Allied decree, IG Farben split into successor companies that quickly reclaimed their positions in the global market. Bayer became a pharmaceutical giant. BASF dominated chemicals. Hoechst expanded into dyes and industrial materials. Their leadership, though altered, often included figures who had weathered the transition with the subtlety of seasoned diplomats.

Or look to the Ruhr industrial region, where coal, steel, and heavy manufacturing formed the backbone of the German economy. The industrialists there had long-standing ties to bankers in London and New York, connections that survived even the most difficult years of war. As early as 1946, Ruhr executives were advising Allied occupation authorities on the reorganization of their own industries. Their counsel produced policies intended to decentralize power yet paradoxically strengthened the influence of those who understood the system best.

The Red House plan was not a conspiracy in the narrow sense of the word. It was a strategy—a survival instinct sharpened by experience, informed by history, and executed by men who understood that regimes are fragile but networks endure. It revealed a truth older than the war itself. Power is not confined to political structures, but flows through the institutions, relationships, and economic forces that outlast them.

This understanding sculpted the decades that followed. It shaped:

- American intelligence strategy
- European integration
- The creation of supranational institutions
- The Marshall Plan, whose funds flowed into European economics already mapped by the industrial relationships nurtured long before 1944

When American officials marveled at the speed of Germany's postwar recovery, they often missed the deeper story: Germany recovered quickly because its industrial foundation had never been fully dismantled. The groundwork had been laid not in 1947 with the Marshall Plan, but in 1944 at the Maison Rouge.

This truth, long buried in archives and footnotes, helps explain why the economic core of Europe was rebuilt not on new principles but on the old scaffolding of continental industry. It explains the seamless transition from wartime production to postwar prosperity. And it also explains the astonishing rise of companies that seemed to have emerged from ruin with unbroken confidence.

It also explains why the United States—triumphant, idealistic, and committed to shaping a democratic world—found itself quietly aligned with the very networks that had once sustained the Reich.

This alignment was not ideological. It was structural.

To rebuild Europe, the United States needed stability. To achieve stability, it needed the cooperation of industrialists and bankers who understood the European landscape better than any American official. The Red House plan became, in effect, a shadow blueprint for European reconstruction—not because the Allies endorsed it, but because they operated within the architecture it had preserved.

By the time the Federal Republic of Germany was established in 1949, the industrialists who had gathered in Strasbourg five years earlier were no longer exiles in waiting. They were advisors, executives, ministers. The indispensable nature of their expertise was evident in chemicals, engineering, metallurgy, transportation, energy, and telecommunications. Their networks spanning Switzerland, Argentina, Britain, and the United States provided the connective tissue of a reborn German economy.

And their worldview—that stability must outweigh ideology, that industry must survive politics, that capital must remain free to move—became the unspoken foundation of the new Europe.

The Red House legacy did not simply prepare Germany to survive defeat. It prepared Germany to lead again, but in a different register.

This resurrection took a new form: No longer militaristic, no longer territorial, but economic, industrial, and transnational. The influence of German firms spread across the continent, shaping the steel and coal communities that eventually evolved into the European Economic Community, then the European Union. In time, the industrial vision crafted in Strasbourg became the economic architecture of an integrated Europe.

The Allies, preoccupied with Soviet aggression, welcomed this outcome. They needed a strong Germany. They needed an industrial powerhouse. They needed partners who could implement American strategy with European expertise.

Thus, the Red House legacy merged seamlessly with the emerging American world order.

What began as a plan for survival became a pillar of postwar stability.

What began as a contingency became continuity.

What began as an act of preservation became a foundation of the modern global system.

The Maison Rouge meeting is remembered, when it is remembered at all, as a curious footnote of the war. But it is more than that. It is the soft overture to the postwar symphony, a whispered acknowledgment that power does not end when regimes collapse. It migrates. It adapts. It survives in the institutions that can weather political storms, in the networks that transcend ideology, and in the men who understand that history rewards those who prepare for the world to come, not mourn the world that is dying.

It was in Strasbourg, not merely in Berlin, that the seeds of the modern era were planted.

And the architects who gathered there knew, with chilling clarity, that defeat in the present could be leveraged into influence in the future.

Their story is not the story of a dying Reich. It is the story of a world being subtly reorganized.

Friedrich Flick did not attend the Red House meeting in August 1944. He did not need to. By that point, his own preparations for postwar survival were already well advanced. Flick had built the largest private industrial empire in Germany through the 1920s and 1930s, accumulating coal mines, steel plants, and manufacturing concerns across the Reich with a single-mindedness that made him one of the most powerful men in Europe.

Flick's companies had used Jewish slave labor. His coal mines had worked prisoners from the concentration camp system. His steel had gone into the Wehrmacht's guns and the Luftwaffe's airframes. None of this was concealed from the Nuremberg investigators who prosecuted him in 1947.

The Nuremberg Military Tribunal convicted Friedrich Flick on two counts: The use of slave labor and the spoliation of occupied territories. He was sentenced to seven years in prison. He served three. In January 1951, John J. McCloy, exercising his authority as U.S. High Commissioner for Germany, commuted the sentences of Flick and fifteen other industrialists convicted at Nuremberg, citing their advanced age and poor health. Flick was fifty-eight. He was photographed leaving Landsberg Prison in a business suit, while carrying a briefcase.

Within four years, he had reconstituted his industrial empire. By 1955, Friedrich Flick was the wealthiest private individual in West Germany. His companies employed 40,000 people. His coal and steel operations supplied the industrial base of the German economic miracle. He maintained no public profile, gave no interviews, and made no acknowledgment of the history that had made him wealthy the first time. He died at age ninety, in 1972, as one of the wealthiest men in Europe, having paid not a single mark in reparations to the survivors of his forced labor programs.

His estate was divided among his heirs.

The Red House legacy did not require ideology to endure. It required only the willingness of the postwar order to look away—and the men who administered that order provided exactly that.

–CHAPTER THREE–

THE ARCHITECTS

> *"For you see, the world is governed by very different personages from what is imagined by those who are not behind the scenes."*
>
> BENJAMIN DISRAELI

THE ARCHITECTURE OF THE modern world did not emerge from treaties or elections, nor from the thunder of battlefield victories. It emerged from rooms where the lights were dim, the curtains drawn, and the doors guarded by silence. In the decade between 1944 and 1954, as the world staggered from the ruins of one order into the birth pains of another, a group of men moved quietly through those rooms, shaping the foundations of the world that would replace the one in ash.

They were not visionaries in the romantic sense, nor ideologues with manifestos tucked under their arms. They were architects of continuity—men who understood that while wars shatter governments, they rarely shatter the forces beneath them: Capital, expertise, networks, and the machinery of influence. These men did not simply adapt to the postwar era; they defined it. Their fingerprints can be found on the creation of the CIA, on the reconstitution of German industry, on the formation of the United Nations (UN) and the Bretton Woods institutions, on the reconstruction of Europe, and on the quiet emergence of a global order that spoke the language of cooperation even as it consolidated power.

To understand the decade, one must understand them.

And to understand them, one must begin not in Washington or London, but in the years before the war: In the paneled offices of Wall Street law firms, in the discreet salons of Geneva, in the counting rooms of Basel, and in the drafting chambers of corporate empires whose holdings spanned continents.

If the Red House meeting revealed how German industrialists prepared for the transition from defeat to resurrection, then the story of the architects reveals how American and British elites prepared to guide—not merely rebuild—the postwar world. Their motivations were varied: Some feared Soviet expansion, some believed in the promise of internationalism, and others simply recognized that in crisis lay opportunity. But their convergence created an alignment so powerful and so seamless that it would define the global system for generations.

The figure who best embodies this convergence is Allen Dulles, a man whose career arcs across the century like a shadow, linking the world before the war to the world that followed. When the bombs fell on London and Paris, Dulles did not rush to the front lines; he slipped into Bern, the tranquil Swiss enclave whose neutrality made it the nerve center of wartime intrigue. There, in a modest villa on the Herrengasse, he presided over a web of informants, industrial liaisons, bankers, defectors, and intermediaries whose allegiance lay not to ideology but to alignment. Dulles understood early what many in Washington did not: That war creates chaos, and chaos creates opportunity for those who know how to navigate its complexity.

The networks he built in Switzerland spanned enemy lines. He met with German officers who saw the Reich's collapse approaching and sought guarantees for their future. He communicated with industrialists whose businesses had been entangled with the Nazi regime but whose expertise would be indispensable in any postwar order. He cultivated relationships with bankers who possessed the one thing that survived every political shift: *Liquidity*.

Dulles was not a rogue agent; he was an architect recognizing the future shape of power. And he was not alone.

His brother, John Foster Dulles, moved through Washington with the same subtlety, crafting diplomatic frameworks that would bind nations to agreements whose implications extended far beyond the immediate crisis. A partner at Sullivan & Cromwell, Dulles had spent the interwar years stitching together agreements for international corporations whose influence rivaled that of governments. He understood that capital flowed more easily across borders than armies ever could, and that whoever controlled the architecture of global finance would control the world emerging from the ashes.

The Dulles brothers did not invent the postwar order. But they acted as conductors, harmonizing forces that already existed: The ambitions of industrialists, the leverage of banks, the vision of foundations, the expertise of technocrats, the urgency of statesmen determined to avoid another world war. They guided these forces into alignment, constructing a system that would appear cooperative on its surface but would rest on a hidden scaffolding of continuity.

And yet, they were only one aspect of a broader constellation.

The Rockefeller network, perhaps the most influential private empire in the history of the United States, provided intellectual, financial, and institutional infrastructure for the world that would follow. Their foundations did not merely donate; they engineered. They engineered public health systems, agricultural revolutions, academic frameworks, cultural institutions, and foreign policy paradigms. They understood that shaping the world required shaping the minds of those who would lead it.

Through universities, think tanks, and international organizations, they cultivated generations of policymakers fluent in the language of globalism.

Their reach was so extensive, so woven into the fabric of American governance, that it became invisible—the way a foundation becomes invisible once the building rises above it.

But even this does not capture the entire picture.

The central bankers of Basel, perched atop the citadel of the Bank for International Settlements, provided a continuity that transcended politics entirely. The BIS, which had quietly facilitated financial exchanges between Allied and Axis banks during the war, emerged from the conflict not bruised but vindicated. Its defenders—men like Thomas McKittrick—insisted that only a neutral institution, insulated from national pressures, could stabilize the global monetary system. They were not wrong. But their definition of "neutrality" reflected a philosophy that would define the postwar order: Stability above sovereignty, continuity above our democratic republic.

From their vantage point, political change was a variable; monetary continuity was a necessity. So the architects who gathered in Basel saw themselves not as rescuers of an old system but as guardians of a new one.

If Dulles represents intelligence, and Rockefeller represents influence, then Basel represents infrastructure—the invisible infrastructure of flows, exchanges, credits, settlements, and reserves that determines the shape of economies. These forces converged again and again during the decade, in the:

- Marshall Plan's distribution of capital
- Creation of the Central Intelligence Agency (CIA)
- Rapid resurrection of German industry
- Shaping of the United Nations (UN)
- Formation of NATO
- Hushed evolution of the European Coal and Steel Community
- Normalization of intelligence alliances that bypassed legislative oversight

- Creation of legal immunities for international institutions
- Rise of technological research programs that would someday define the digital age

The architects understood that the world after the war could not be left to chance. They understood that ideology, though powerful, was unstable. They understood that the future would belong to those who could navigate complexity, not rhetoric. And they understood that a new kind of governance was emerging; one not defined by borders, but by networks.

Power often survives catastrophe not by brute force but by adaptation. Empires fall, governments collapse, flags are burned, and constitutions rewritten. Yet, the underlying machinery—the habits of influence, the networks of finance, the expertise embedded in institutions—rarely dies with the regimes they serve. It migrates. It conforms to the new landscape. It preserves itself by attaching to whatever structure rises from the rubble. And in the decade after World War II, that machinery found its form in a cadre of men whose influence extended across continents, time zones, and political systems.

To grasp their role, one must step back from the smoke-choked ruins of Europe and examine the deeper strata of the world they were building. These architects were not improvising. They worked from an unwritten blueprint forged long before the war—a blueprint shaped by the rhythms of international finance, the logic of covert diplomacy, the ambitions of multinational corporations, and the belief that sovereignty was too unstable a force to ensure global order.

In Washington, this blueprint took shape in the hands of men who had spent their formative years advising the very industrial and financial concerns that helped fuel the rise of totalitarian regimes. To them, the world was not divided into good nations and bad nations, victors and vanquished. It was divided into three systems: 1) those that worked, 2) those that failed, and 3) those that could be redirected. They believed history rewarded the pragmatic, not the sentimental. And in the turbulence of the 1940s, they saw the opportunity of a century.

Allen Dulles embodied this principle with almost uncanny precision. His wartime post in Bern gave him a vantage point few intelligence officers ever acquired: A front-row seat not only to the collapse of the Reich, but to the quiet negotiations that would shape what followed. Bern became a peculiar kind of crucible—a city where couriers disappeared into cafés with coded messages, where industrialists from defeated nations sought absolution through cooperation, where ministers from neutral states whispered of what might emerge when the guns fell silent.

Dulles did not simply collect information; he curated networks. He met with German bankers who understood the importance of preserving assets that could be mobilized in a postwar reconstruction. He cultivated scientists who dreaded Soviet captivity more than American scrutiny. He corresponded with industrialists who had no intention of allowing the destruction of Berlin or the indictments of Nuremberg to sever the lifelines of their empires. And through each relationship, each carefully phrased assurance, each discreet act of facilitation, he wove a fabric of continuity that would outlast the very governments whose collapse had enabled it.

This sensibility resonated strongly with the elite circles from which he came—circles where law firms doubled as diplomatic channels, where foundations shaped policy beneath the veneer of philanthropy, and where corporate alliances transcended borders more fluidly than any treaty. Sullivan & Cromwell, the Dulles brothers' professional birthplace, was more than a law firm. It was a crucible of internationalist philosophy, a place where the intricacies of global finance were not abstractions but the practical tools of influence.

Through its corridors passed the architects of the postwar order: Men who had advised German cartels, arranged the financing of oil empires, mediated disputes between European states, and shaped the doctrines that would guide the international institutions to come.

And standing just beyond that doorway, operating on a broader canvas but with the same structural instincts, was the Rockefeller dynasty—perhaps the most consequential private force in twentieth-century geopolitics. The Rockefellers possessed a rare combination of resources: Immense financial capital, expansive philanthropic infrastructure, global reach, and a coherent worldview about the future of civilization. They believed modernity required coordination, that peace required interdependence, and that the United States, emerging from the war as the world's economic heart, had a responsibility to engineer a system capable of preventing future catastrophes.

John D. Rockefeller Jr., and later his sons, invested heavily not merely in institutions but in ideas. Their foundations funded global health initiatives, agricultural revolutions, and academic institutions. But beneath these efforts ran a deeper purpose: Constructing an intellectual and administrative elite aligned with the principles of international governance. They understood that influence was not secured by control alone, but by shaping the assumptions of the people who would eventually wield power.

Thus arose a new intellectual infrastructure: The Council on Foreign Relations, the Rockefeller Foundation, the Ford Foundation, the Harvard and MIT international studies programs, the establishment of UNESCO (The United Nations Educational, Scientific and Cultural Organization), along with the expansion of the UN's development agencies. Each was a strand in a web that stretched outward from Manhattan and Washington toward the capitals of Europe, the emerging postcolonial world, and the developing corridors of the intelligence community.

Yet even these forces, formidable as they were, could not build the postwar world alone. They required the silent ballast of the central bankers, whose philosophies had been formed not by ideology but by crisis—men who viewed stability as the moral imperative of civilization. Their cathedral was the Bank for International Settlements in Basel, a building that had survived the war with barely a scratch, protected by a neutrality that masked its deeper purpose. To these men, borders were abstractions; currencies were the true battleground. They believed inflation could topple governments more effectively than armies, that liquidity could resuscitate economies from collapse, and that monetary coordination was the only path to a durable world system.

Thus emerged the triumvirate that would define the architecture beneath the age:

- The intelligence networks that managed information
- The financial networks that managed capital
- The institutional networks that managed ideology

Each strengthened the others. Each obscured the others.

And together, they created a continuum of influence that could withstand elections, revolutions, and even the temporary setbacks of public scrutiny.

This was not conspiracy. It was continuity.

The quiet inheritance of a world too complex to leave to chance. And as 1947 gave way to 1949, as the Cold War hardened into doctrine, as Europe emerged from rubble into reconstruction, these architects stood ready—not merely to guide the new world, but to design it.

The question was never whether they could.
The question was how far they intended to go.

In the final years of the 1940s, even as the ashes of the war cooled, and the outlines of the Cold War sharpened, an unspoken convergence was drawing together the disparate networks that had survived the upheaval.

What had begun as separate spheres—intelligence, finance, diplomacy, industry, philanthropy—drifted toward a common center of gravity, each reinforcing the other with an ease that suggested inevitability rather than design. But inevitability is often the argument of hindsight.

In the moment itself, the convergence was something more subtle: A recognition among the architects that the world emerging from the ruins could not be left to the improvisations of politics or the passions of the public. It required stewardship, and they believed themselves to be the only ones capable of providing it.

Nowhere was this more apparent than in the institutional corridors of Washington, where the fledgling CIA began to reveal the ambitions embedded in its structure. Though born from wartime intelligence, it was quickly transformed by men like Allen Dulles into an instrument of statecraft whose reach exceeded the boundaries of traditional espionage. Its mandate expanded to include covert operations, economic influence, psychological warfare, and the shaping of political outcomes abroad—activities justified by the growing specter of Soviet expansion. But beneath the rhetoric of containment lay another motivation: The desire to sustain the continuity of the international order being built through the reconstruction of Europe and the integration of global financial systems.

The CIA's emerging culture reflected this dual purpose. Many of its early recruits came from Ivy League institutions, Wall Street partnerships, and philanthropic foundations—men who carried with them an instinctive comfort with transnational networks and an aversion to the unpredictability of democratic politics. They moved through the world with a shared fluency in culture and power, confident in their ability to interpret the moral ambiguities of the Cold War with a steadiness the public lacked. In their hands, intelligence became not merely information gathering, but an instrument for shaping the trajectory of nations in ways that aligned with the architecture being crafted behind the scenes.

This alignment was not accidental. It grew from the intimate overlap between the intelligence community and the financial families who were steering the reconstruction of Europe. The Rockefellers, whose philanthropic endeavors offered a veneer of benevolence to their strategic interests, maintained close ties with policymakers and intelligence officers. Their funding manipulated the intellectual climate of universities and think tanks. Their involvement in international development underscored the belief that American expansion and global stability were mutually reinforcing. And their relationships with European industrialists, many of whom had weathered the war with their networks intact, helped coordinate the flow of capital and expertise necessary to rebuild the continent.

These connections extended into the legal world as well, where firms like Sullivan & Cromwell operated as the soft infrastructure of postwar diplomacy. The firm's partners, including the Dulles brothers, had spent decades representing multinational corporations whose fortunes depended on a stable international environment. They understood the intricacies of global commerce and the vulnerabilities of economic interdependence. Their legal work often blurred into geopolitical strategy, as they advised governments, mediated disputes, and facilitated alliances that reinforced the emerging world order. And as their influence grew, so did the coherence of the architecture they helped craft.

Meanwhile, the BIS continued its quiet work in Basel, coordinating the financial policies of central banks through discreet consultations and unpublicized agreements. Its meetings, attended by men who viewed currency stability as the cornerstone of civilization, were conducted in an atmosphere of calm deliberation that belied the tensions of the era.

They discussed inflation, liquidity, exchange rates, and the mechanisms of cross-border payments with clarity and detachment that would have been unthinkable in the volatile political climate of the 1930s. And through these discussions, they reinforced the belief that monetary governance required insulation from democratic pressures. This belief would become a defining feature of the postwar economy.

Industrialists, too, played their part in the convergence. In Germany, the dismantling of the cartels that had supported the Reich was carried out with a pragmatism that revealed the underlying continuity of the system. Many of the same executives who had guided wartime production returned to positions of influence in the postwar economy, their knowledge and relationships deemed indispensable to the reconstruction effort. Their companies, restructured and rebranded, became pillars of the new European industrial order.

And as they integrated into multinational markets, they forged alliances with American corporations that further knitted the transatlantic economy together.

Even the philanthropic world, ostensibly removed from the machinations of power, became an essential component of the architecture. Foundations funded research into international law, economic development, and social science, shaping the intellectual paradigms that would guide policymakers for decades.

They supported cultural and educational exchanges that fostered a sense of global citizenship among the rising generation. They sponsored initiatives in public health, agriculture, and urban planning that aligned with the economic priorities of governments and corporations. And through these efforts, they helped cultivate a worldview that saw global integration not merely as beneficial, but as necessary.

What emerged from this convergence was a system that possessed the characteristics of an empire without the explicit trappings of imperial rule. It had no emperor, no central capital, no official doctrine. Yet it wielded extraordinary influence through the coordination of institutions whose mandates extended across borders and whose authority derived from their technical expertise rather than electoral legitimacy. It was a velvet empire, soft in its presentation but firm in its structure, capable of shaping the decisions of nations while remaining largely invisible to their citizens.

History has a way of revealing what was once hidden.

This invisibility was its strength—and its vulnerability. Although the architects believed they were acting in the best interests of global stability, their methods often bypassed the democratic processes that were meant to govern the postwar world. They assumed that the public, preoccupied with the demands of daily life, would accept the arrangements they crafted without question. And for a time, this assumption held. The prosperity of the early Cold War years masked the deeper shifts taking place beneath the surface, and the narrative of ideological rivalry between East and West provided a convenient justification for actions that might otherwise have provoked scrutiny.

But history has a way of revealing what was once hidden.

And as the 1950s progressed, the foundations of the architecture began to solidify in ways that made their presence undeniable.

–CHAPTER FOUR–

OPERATION PAPERCLIP

"Science has no fatherland."

LOUIS PASTEUR

THE WAR HAD NOT yet finished dying when the world's future began to pivot quietly in another direction, away from the ruins and treaties, away even from the military winners and losers. It pivoted instead through a corridor of decisions that were never meant to be recorded, through meetings whose participants would later describe them only vaguely, and through a moral terrain so unsettled that even those who walked it spoke in the language of necessity rather than conviction. It was in this space—between victory and uncertainty, between what the world believed and what its new custodians feared—that Operation Paperclip was born.

The public, exhausted by years of loss, believed the war had been fought and won for reasons as old as civilization: To defeat tyranny, to liberate the oppressed, to reclaim the dignity of nations. Yet for those working inside American intelligence, a far more complex picture was already forming. They understood that wars do not end cleanly. They understood that regimes collapse suddenly, but their knowledge does not evaporate. And they understood that in the dawning Cold War—a conflict not yet named but already taking shape—knowledge would become the most valuable currency in the world.

The Reich, for all its monstrous crimes, had achieved scientific and technological breakthroughs at a pace unmatched by any Allied nation. It had poured immense resources into rocketry, aerodynamics, chemical and biological experimentation, cryptography, advanced metallurgy, signal intelligence, and the dark corners of human behavior. It had created laboratories that lived outside the constraints of morality, staffed by men who believed their allegiance to science justified any method. Now, with Germany collapsing and Soviet armies racing westward, the United States faced a stark truth: The future would belong not to the nation with the best morals, but to the nation with the best minds.

The earliest conversations about recruiting former Nazi scientists were hesitant, almost tentative, framed in the language of exploration rather than strategy. But as reports filtered in from the European fronts, detailing abandoned research programs, half-finished weapons systems, untested prototypes, and scientists willing to barter knowledge for freedom, hesitation gave way to urgency. Intelligence officers recognized that the Soviets, too, were hunting these men. The race for the future had begun long before the guns fell silent.

Allen Dulles, observing all of this from his post in Bern, understood the stakes with forensic clarity. His wartime intelligence network had exposed him to the arcane world of German research; he knew which laboratories mattered, which scientists were indispensable, and which industrialists could facilitate their extraction. He saw the chaos of collapse not as an ending, but as a window. It was a moment when the world's most dangerous knowledge could be seized, redirected, and repurposed in the service of a new order.

Yet Paperclip was not merely an intelligence program. It was, as Annie Jacobsen reminds us in her book, *Operation Paperclip,* a moral test disguised as a logistical operation, a negotiation between what was expedient and what was righteous. And as the operation grew, that negotiation tilted decisively toward expedience.

The men at the center of this program—Wernher von Braun, Arthur Rudolph, Hubertus Strughold, Walter Schreiber, and hundreds more—represented the full spectrum of scientific brilliance and ethical ruin. Some had worked on the V-2 rockets that terrorized London; others had overseen medical experiments whose cruelty defied imagination. Still others were embedded in industrial networks that had sustained the Reich's war machine. Their personal histories were often entangled with SS affiliations, forced labor programs, and projects that violated every principle the Allies had professed to defend.

One by one, their pasts were laundered through a meticulous bureaucratic process designed to make them fit for American service. Intelligence officers rewrote dossiers, sanitized files, removed incriminating evidence, and recast these men as apolitical specialists swept along by history. The logic was presented as unassailable: If America did not rescue these scientists, the Soviets would. And if the Soviets acquired them, the world's balance of power would tilt dangerously eastward.

The Rockefellers and their philanthropic network understood the implications instantly. They recognized that scientific supremacy would shape not only military power but economic direction, industrial innovation, global governance, and the ideological future of entire societies. Their foundations quietly supported early aerospace initiatives, university research programs, and international scientific collaborations that absorbed Paperclip personnel into the bloodstream of American technological advancement. Through grants, fellowships, and institutional partnerships, they helped construct an intellectual superstructure in which the scientists of the former Reich became architects of the new American century.

What emerged was a paradox—a nation that had defeated fascism by absorbing its scientific legacy. Our republic had preserved its future by compromising its past. Paperclip was not simply a transfer of expertise. It was a transference of worldview, a silent migration of ideas, methods, and notions from a defeated regime into the administrative fabric of the victor.

Some of these men contributed to the rockets that would send Americans to the moon. Others shaped the chemical and aviation industries that powered the Cold War economy. Still others influenced intelligence programs, psychological operations, and research into the manipulation of the human mind. In these areas, the lines between innovation and violation blurred to an uncomfortable degree.

The American public, told only that the war had been won and peace restored, had little understanding of the moral ambiguities unfolding behind closed doors. They saw the rapid technological progress of the 1950s, including the satellites, the jet engines, and the medical breakthroughs, and assumed it was the natural fruit of American genius. They worshipped the clean geometry of rockets, the sleek promise of the space age, the dream of a future without the shadow of war.

But the future was not as clean as the rockets suggested.

Paperclip had changed America, not only scientifically, but philosophically. It had introduced a new ethic into the bloodstream of national policy: The belief that ends justify means, that secrecy is sometimes virtue, that expertise can absolve history, and that the management of global power occasionally requires moral concessions unseen and unchosen by the public.

And this ethic aligned perfectly with the broader architecture being built by the Dulles brothers, the Rockefellers, the BIS, and the transnational networks whose influence stretched far beyond electoral scrutiny. In a sense, Paperclip did more than bring Nazi scientists to America. It brought America further into the world they had helped envision, a world where sovereignty was malleable, where secrecy was a tool of governance, where elite networks molded the future in rooms without windows.

The story of Paperclip is not merely the story of scientists rescued from the ruins of the Reich. It is the story of how the postwar order absorbed the very forces it claimed to have defeated, weaving them into a new tapestry of power that would define the decades ahead.

And as the 1950s unfolded, the operation's consequences would reach far beyond laboratories and launchpads.

They would shape intelligence doctrines, inform industrial policy, accelerate the Cold War, and redefine the boundaries of what their democracy would tolerate in the name of survival.

This was the silent bargain of the postwar world. And its cost had only begun to reveal itself.

If the first phase of Operation Paperclip unfolded in the shadows of collapsing German laboratories, the second phase unfolded amid the bright, orderly optimism of postwar America—a contrast so stark it almost seems like two different worlds. Yet the men who stepped off military transport planes into the crisp midwestern air, escorted by officers who barely spoke above a whisper, understood that they were crossing not simply a geographic boundary, but a moral one. They knew that their pasts were not being erased, but repurposed; not denied, but reinterpreted in ways that suited the geopolitical realities of the moment.

The United States, flush with victory yet unprepared for the scale of scientific rivalry about to define the century, had made an extraordinary choice: It would absorb the minds that had helped build Hitler's war machine, not as prisoners or pariahs, but as instruments of a new American ascendancy. The nation that had condemned the horrors of the Reich now quietly enlisted the very men who had advanced its technological ambitions. It was a decision that would ripple through the corridors of military research, the nascent aerospace industry, the intelligence community, and eventually the deepest realms of the American psyche.

The soldiers who guarded the first Paperclip transports often spoke later of the unease they felt—an unease born not of fear, but of contradiction. These transports were the men whose work had reduced parts of Europe to rubble, whose rockets had torn through the night sky above London, whose medical units had conducted experiments in camps Americans could barely imagine. Yet here they were, sitting on canvas seats, staring out at the unfamiliar horizon of a country that had defeated them, a country that would now shelter them, fund them, and many times elevate them to positions of extraordinary influence.

Wernher von Braun, brilliant and charming, embodied this contradiction with a kind of effortless grace. He smiled easily, spoke fluidly, and carried himself with the air of a man who had always known he would land on his feet.

Von Braun had been to Dora-Mittelbau, an underground factory in the Harz Mountains, which was not a peripheral element of his program. It was its production heart where the V-2 rockets were built in tunnels carved from rock by concentration camp prisoners working twelve-hour shifts in conditions of deliberate brutality. Approximately 20,000 prisoners died at Dora and its satellite camps between 1943 and 1945 from overwork, malnutrition, beatings, and summary execution.

Wernher von Braun visited the facility at least once. Former prisoners testified to his presence. His later account held that he had been unaware of the conditions under which his rockets were built—an account that the facility's own documentation did not support.

None of this appeared in the dossier that American intelligence prepared for his entry into the United States. The officers who cleared Wernher von Braun for Operation Paperclip knew what was in the full files. They chose what to forward and what to retain. His SS membership—he held the rank of Sturmbannführer, roughly equivalent to major—was noted and set aside. The slave labor question was classified as a personnel matter of the previous employer.

He arrived at Fort Bliss, Texas, in September 1945, and was welcomed with the deference owed to a visiting academic. Over the next three decades, he became the public face of American space ambition, a man whose charm and vision genuinely moved the engineers who worked beside him. He received the National Medal of Science from Richard Nixon in 1969, the year Americans walked on the moon.

The distance between Dora-Mittelbau and the Rose Garden ceremony at the Nixon White House was the distance Paperclip traveled. It is also the distance the postwar order asked the public not to measure.

To the officers escorting him, he seemed less like a vanquished enemy than a visiting dignitary—a perception that unsettled anyone who had seen the photographs of Dora-Mittelbau or read the testimonies of those who had survived it. Von Braun was welcomed into military laboratories with little more than a handshake and the quiet removal of a few inconvenient paperwork references.

Others followed similarly strange paths. Hubertus Strughold, whose research into aviation medicine had depended on experiments conducted in freezing chambers and low-pressure altitudes, was absorbed into the American aerospace medical program, eventually hailed as the "Father of Space Medicine." Walter Dornberger, who had directed the V-2 program with an unwavering loyalty to the Reich, found a new home in American corporate defense work. Kurt Debus, who had overseen V-2 launches from sites where slave laborers died by the thousands, would later preside over America's first manned spaceflight launch center.

Rogue officers or clandestine factions did not oversee these transformations. They were sanctioned at the highest levels of the emerging national security apparatus. The logic was always articulated with clinical precision: The Cold War demanded superiority in every domain, and superiority demanded expertise—even tainted expertise. The Soviets, it was argued, would have no qualms using these men. Therefore, America could not afford the luxury of conscience.

The Dulles brothers, though not the official stewards of Paperclip, understood its deeper significance instinctively. For Allen, whose wartime intelligence work had taught him the value of networks over ideologies, Paperclip offered not only scientific leverage but an opportunity to reshape the American intelligence landscape. For John Foster, who viewed international relations through the lens of corporate diplomacy and global strategy, the operation reinforced his conviction that the postwar order would depend more on technological supremacy and economic integration than on moral clarity.

Behind them stood the philanthropic and industrial networks that helped shape "Scientific America"—the vision of a nation whose power would be defined by the ability to innovate, to build, to engineer solutions to geopolitical dilemmas. The Rockefeller Foundation funded research programs that drew Paperclip scientists into the academic and technical mainstream. Aerospace contractors lobbied for access to their knowledge. Universities, hungry for prestige and government contracts, provided institutional homes that allowed these men to shed their pasts like old uniforms.

Yet for all the institutions working to integrate these scientists, none played a more complex role than the intelligence community. It was the intelligence officers who sanitized files, redirected investigations, and constructed the official narratives that justified the recruitment. They assembled dossiers that omitted entire chapters of history, reframed war crimes as unfortunate necessities, and presented the scientists as reluctant participants caught in the tides of authoritarianism. In doing so, they reshaped not only the biographies of these men but the very boundaries of what America was willing to accept in the name of national security.

This reframing had consequences far beyond the laboratories. It established a precedent—one that would quietly influence American foreign policy, intelligence operations, and scientific research for decades. The precedent was simple: Secrecy could be used not only to protect the nation but to shield its actions from the moral scrutiny of its own citizens. Paperclip taught America that technical expertise could be prioritized over ethical accountability, that national survival could be invoked to justify decisions that might otherwise seem unthinkable.

And so, as the 1950s unfolded, Paperclip cast a long shadow, one that stretched from the deserts of New Mexico to the laboratories of Dayton, from the aerospace corridors of Huntsville to the intelligence enclaves of Washington. It created the early space race, influenced the development of psychological warfare programs, and contributed to the ethos of secrecy that defined the Cold War. It altered the trajectory of American science, transforming the nation from a wartime industrial power into a technological superpower.

But perhaps its most lasting impact was not technological at all. It was philosophical.

Paperclip normalized the idea that democratic societies could make decisions of profound ethical consequence without public debate. It taught the emerging National Security State that the management of knowledge—the careful curation of what the public was permitted to know—was as crucial to governance as the management of resources or alliances. It blurred the distinction between victory and absorption, between defeating an enemy and becoming entangled in its legacy.

Paperclip was not merely an operation. It was a transformation.

In this way, Paperclip was not merely an operation. It was a transformation. It altered America's moral geography, redefining the boundaries of what was permissible in the name of survival. And it did so quietly, subtly, with a precision that mirrored the engineering brilliance of the men it had recruited.

The world that emerged from this transformation—a world defined by secrecy, technological rivalry, and transnational networks of expertise—was not the world the public believed it had fought to preserve. It was, instead, the world its leaders believed was necessary to navigate the uncertainties of the new age.

And in the years ahead, this world would grow only more complex, more interconnected, and more elusive—a world where sovereignty could be circumvented without a single shot fired, and where the most consequential battles would be fought not on land or sea, but in laboratories, intelligence briefings, and the sealed chambers of international institutions.

Operation Paperclip had revealed a truth the architects understood from the beginning:

> **In the modern age, the most powerful invasions are those that never announce themselves.**

For all the logistical complexity of transporting hundreds of scientists across the Atlantic, the true weight of Operation Paperclip was carried not in crates of documents or prototypes but in the still, unspoken reckoning that unfolded inside the American institutions absorbing them. There was a point, somewhere between the end of the war and the solidification of the Cold War, when the meaning of victory blurred.

It was as if the nation had stepped into a twilight where the lines between necessity and compromise could no longer be distinguished without squinting.

In this twilight, the scientists lived parallel lives—one recorded in their American resumes, another buried in the sealed archives of their past. In their new positions, they wore crisp uniforms and carried identification cards embossed with American emblems, the bureaucratic symbols of belonging. They walked through laboratories that gleamed with the promise of a better world. These laboratories were filled with young American engineers and physicists who viewed them as mentors, pioneers, even heroes. But beneath the veneer of mentorship was a ghostly thread that connected these men to rooms where human suffering had been commodified in the name of progress.

The Americans who supervised Paperclip navigated this contradiction with the language of strategy. They spoke of Soviet advancements, of nuclear brinkmanship, of the need to stay ahead. They cited intelligence estimates forecasting a world divided into spheres of influence, each defined not by geography but by scientific potential. They reminded themselves—and each other—that this was not a war of armies but of ideas, materials, and acceleration. And in this calculus, the sins of the past were reframed as the cost of the present.

But the moral reckoning they hoped to postpone did not disappear. It settled into the cultural air of the era like invisible dust—undetectable, yet present in every decision that followed. It seeped into the psychology of institutions, shaping how they approached secrecy, accountability, and the ethics of power. It influenced the way Americans thought about progress, creating a subtle but profound tension between the nation's democratic ideals and the opaque structures emerging behind them.

Within the intelligence community, this tension played out in the debates that surrounded early mind and behavior research. Inspired by whispers of Soviet experiments, American officials sought ways to understand and potentially influence the human psyche. Some of these efforts were benign, grounded in psychology and social science.

Others drifted into darker territory. This research drew on the knowledge of Paperclip scientists whose wartime work had blurred, if not erased, the boundary between experimentation and violation.

It was in these domains that the true legacy of Paperclip revealed itself. For the operation had done more than import expertise; it had imported a worldview—one that positioned scientific ambition above moral restraint, one that accepted secrecy as a form of necessity, one that saw the individual not as an autonomous being but as a variable in the equation of national survival.

This worldview resonated with the emerging national security apparatus, whose leaders saw the preservation of the American-led order as a mission that transcended the constraints of ordinary governance. They believed the world was entering a period of unprecedented instability, a contest between two systems of power that demanded flexibility, improvisation, and rapid decision-making. They believed that transparency was a luxury, not a doctrine. And they believed that the public, shielded from the most complex elements of geopolitics, would accept the outcomes of decisions they never knew had been made.

In this sense, Paperclip became a template—a demonstration that the United States could operate in worlds beyond public view, that it could make choices of extraordinary consequence without democratic input, that it could hold contradictions without collapsing under their weight. It taught the intelligence community that secrets could serve as structural supports, that the public need not understand the machinery of protection to benefit from its output.

But it also taught the architects something else—something they did not articulate but carried with them nonetheless: That the line between preserving the vision of democracy and managing it is perilously thin.

Meanwhile, in laboratories across the country, the scientists who had arrived through Paperclip were beginning to reshape American technological identity. They introduced a precision of engineering that had been honed under the pressures of authoritarian command structures—a precision that now drove the nascent space program, missile development, advanced aviation, and chemical research. Their influence extended not only through the devices they built but through the attitudes they fostered among the Americans who worked beside them.

Young engineers in Huntsville, Dayton, and White Sands learned to think in terms of velocity curves, combustion equations, and launch windows. But they also learned to think in terms of strategic imperatives, geopolitical stakes, and the importance of secrecy. For them, the Cold War was not merely ideological; it was a race of materials, designs, and breakthroughs. Every calculation, every test flight, every prototype carried the unspoken weight of a global contest whose contours were defined not by diplomats but by engineers.

Paperclip, in this way, was not merely the importation of expertise; it was the symbiosis of two scientific cultures—one democratic, one authoritarian—each reshaping the other in subtle ways. America offered its scientists the freedom to innovate, the resources to explore, and the optimism of a nation that believed in boundless possibilities. The Paperclip scientists, in turn, offered America the discipline of total war research, the relentless pursuit of optimization, and the belief that technological supremacy could secure national destiny.

This symbiosis produced extraordinary breakthroughs, but it also embedded a paradox in the national psyche—the belief that progress could exist independently of morality. It was a paradox that would surface again in MK-Ultra, in covert coups, in economic experiments conducted on distant nations, and in intelligence operations that stretched the boundaries of democratic consent.

And yet, through it all, the American public remained largely unaware of the bargain that had been struck in their name. They saw the triumphs—the early rockets rising in bright parabolas over the desert, the space-age visions of the 1950s, the assurances of leaders who spoke of

American exceptionalism—but not the shadows beneath them. They celebrated the symbols without understanding the scaffolding.

It was a silence the architects welcomed.

For in the architecture they were building, silence was not an absence but a tool—the space in which power could operate without interference, where the complexities of global management could be distilled into actions unburdened by public deliberation.

Operation Paperclip had not only secured America's minds that would guide its ascent; it had laid the psychological foundation for a new mode of governance, one where sovereignty could be protected by secrecy, where its democracy could be defended by decisions made outside its processes, and where the future could be engineered by a small cadre of men who believed they alone understood the stakes.

The operation, in this last sense, was not a chapter of history.

It was a portal—the threshold through which the United States stepped into an entirely new conception of power.

–CHAPTER FIVE–

INFILTRATION OF THE MIND

> *"Power is in tearing human minds to pieces and putting them together again in new shapes of your own choosing."*
> GEORGE ORWELL

LONG BEFORE THE PUBLIC knew the term "Cold War" and long before the first missile silos were poured or the first satellites traced faint arcs across the night sky, the men shaping the emerging postwar world had already identified the battlefield that would matter most. It would not be waged in trenches or along frozen frontiers. It would not be fought in the skies above Berlin or the deserts of the Middle East. It would unfold in a far more intimate and uncharted territory: The human mind.

This realization did not come suddenly. It emerged gradually, in the dim corridors of intelligence stations, in the academic departments quietly reshaped by foundation money, in the debriefings of Paperclip scientists whose wartime experiments had pushed the boundaries of conscience. It emerged in the shifting priorities of policymakers who understood that power in the twentieth century would no longer rely solely on armies or industries, but on perception—on the management of belief, memory, identity, fear, and desire.

In the decade between 1944 and 1954, a profound change unfolded, one that would shape not only Cold War strategy but the very fabric of modern society. It was a change born from the lessons of Nazi propaganda, Soviet indoctrination, psychological warfare experiments, the trauma of global conflict, and the dawning awareness that entire populations could be steered not by force, but by suggestion.

This was the beginning of the infiltration of the human mind.

It began quietly, intellectually, almost academically. Universities that had once been bastions of pure scholarship found themselves courted by intelligence agencies, foundations, and government departments eager to understand the mechanisms of influence. The Rockefeller Foundation funded studies into human behavior, social psychology, and mass communication. The OSS, and later the CIA, recruited professors and graduate students into projects whose stated purposes were scholarly but whose implications were unmistakably strategic.

Harvard, Yale, MIT, Stanford, and Columbia each became a node in a growing network of psychological research that blurred the line between science and statecraft. The emerging field of "behavioral science," adorned with the prestige of academia, provided a language that could translate the old ambitions of empire into the new vocabulary of influence. Terms like "conditioning," "suggestibility," "cognitive dissonance," and "mass persuasion" drifted from academic journals into intelligence memos.

The men who steered this transformation, many of them trained during wartime psychological operations, understood that the war had revealed an unsettling truth: People could be shaped. Their fears could be directed, their loyalties cultivated, their perceptions engineered with remarkable precision. The Reich had weaponized propaganda with terrifying effectiveness. The Soviets had constructed a state built on ideological indoctrination. And the Allies, for all their victory, recognized that moral outrage alone could not inoculate the public against manipulation.

The war had revealed an unsettling truth: People could be shaped.

If anything, the opposite was true.

The trauma of war made minds more malleable—eager for stability, susceptible to authority, hungry for narratives that restored coherence to a world shattered by conflict.

American intelligence analysts studied Nazi propaganda films frame by frame, dissecting the cinematic techniques that stirred crowds into frenzied devotion. They examined the structure of Soviet education, noting how repetition, ritual, and fear could produce obedience without visible coercion. They scrutinized the psychological profiles of wartime leaders, searching for patterns in charisma, persuasion, and mass influence.

The goal was not to replicate tyranny. It was to understand how tyranny had worked—and to prevent its return. At least, that was the stated purpose.

But beneath that purpose, a quieter ambition began to take shape: If America was to manage the world, as the architects envisioned, then it needed to understand not only how nations behaved, but how individuals did—how they formed beliefs, how they resisted ideas, how they reacted to uncertainty. And this understanding could not be obtained solely through diplomacy or espionage. It required the tools of psychology, sociology, anthropology, and communication theory.

The foundations stepped in to supply the resources. The intelligence agencies supplied the urgency. And the universities supplied the expertise.

By 1947, the landscape of American thought was shifting. Academic departments redesigned curricula around research relevant to national security. Graduate fellowships were quietly funded by agencies whose names did not appear on the checks. Scholars published work that advanced the study of persuasion, group behavior, and ideological resilience—work that later found its way into training manuals and policy briefs.

The infiltration of the mind went beyond academia. It entered the bloodstream of culture itself.

In the early 1950s, American media underwent a transformation so subtle that few recognized its purpose. Films that celebrated American ideals were crafted with the cooperation of the Pentagon. Radio broadcasts carried messaging that framed the U.S. as the stabilizing force in a world threatened by chaos. Newspapers, often unknowingly, ran stories fed through channels built during the war. The newly emerging medium of television—intimate, immersive, and profoundly influential—became an unspoken battleground for narrative control.

And beneath all of this, in laboratories funded through classified budgets, the CIA pursued experiments that pushed psychology into territory where ethics strained to keep hold. Mind and behavior research, no longer limited to observation or theory, expanded into active manipulation. Some programs, like those later associated with MK-Ultra, explored the limits of memory, willpower, and identity. Others studied how sensory deprivation, hypnosis, and trauma might open cracks in the mind through which suggestion could travel.

It is impossible to overstate how radical this shift was. The United States, a nation built on the belief in individual autonomy and the sanctity of conscience, was now exploring methods to penetrate those very foundations. And though many of the officials involved believed they were acting defensively, their work opened avenues of influence that extended far beyond their initial intentions.

And from understanding came imitation.

The logic was always the same: If the Soviets could *do* it, America must *understand* it.

By the early 1950s, the infiltration of the mind had become not a program but a paradigm. It was a way of thinking about power that fused psychology with geopolitics, information with authority, and science with administration.

If the nineteenth century belonged to industrialists, and the early twentieth to financiers, the mid-twentieth belonged to the engineers of belief. But the consequences of this transformation did not remain confined to military strategy or psychological research. They seeped into the cultural, political, and economic life of the nation. Advertising adopted the methods of persuasion pioneered in intelligence research. Political campaigns embraced the psychology of mass influence. Public education began to reflect the globalist ideology funded by foundations. And the public, unaware that the infrastructure of thought itself had shifted, absorbed these changes as naturally as air.

The infiltration of the mind had begun as a response to war. It became the architecture of peace. It was a peace managed through perception, stability maintained through narrative, and identity formed through institutions that operated far from public view.

And as the decade advanced, this architecture would intersect with the rising power of multinational foundations and international institutions, forming a triad of influence that would define the modern world.

The next movement in this story begins with the institutions that funded the architects of perception: The foundations of influence.

The foundations had long presented themselves as engines of philanthropy—benevolent institutions dedicated to curing disease, expanding education, reducing poverty, and advancing global understanding. But in the decade after the war, these organizations became something more complex, more consequential, and far more intertwined with the statecraft of the new American century. They were not conspiratorial bodies, nor were they puppeteers. They were, instead, something subtler and more enduring: Architects of intellectual climate, custodians of globalist ideology, and midwives to a new form of influence that operated through culture, knowledge, and perception rather than through armies or monarchs.

No institution exemplified this transformation more completely than the Rockefeller Foundation. Its philanthropy, always substantial, now stretched across continents, funding agricultural revolutions in Mexico and India, supporting public health campaigns from Cairo to Manila, underwriting academic departments that would become the intellectual DNA of modern social science. Yet beneath these humanitarian efforts lay a coherent worldview: That interconnected problems required interconnected solutions, that expertise, not democratic debate, should shape global systems, and that the United States, as the postwar superpower, bore a responsibility to design and administer the emerging international order.

The foundation's influence extended into universities where young scholars, eager for funding and prestige, found themselves guided toward research that supported the logic of interdependence and international administration. Grants flowed to studies on population control, global governance, international education, psychological resilience, and developmental economics. These were all fields that would become pillars of the global architecture in the decades to come. These academic currents, though often framed in neutral or technical language, carried within them an implicit belief that national sovereignty was increasingly obsolete, a relic of a world before interconnected crises demanded coordinated response.

This intellectual shift was not imposed;
It was cultivated.

It was not declared; it was demonstrated.

It was not argued; it was assumed.

Meanwhile, the Ford and Carnegie foundations, endowed with immense resources and driven by trustees who viewed the world through similar lenses, expanded the reach of this emerging paradigm. They funded the postwar reconstruction of European universities, supported international exchange programs, built networks of scholars who would shape foreign policy, and permeated areas of global development previously untouched by private American institutions.

They sponsored conferences where economists, diplomats, scientists, and bureaucrats gathered to sketch the outlines of a world managed through cooperation, coordination, and expertise. These gatherings were not ideological in the conventional sense. They were managerial—entirely devoted to designing systems that would endure beyond the passions of electoral politics.

As these foundations expanded their global influence, they formed a discreet symbiosis with the intelligence community. The CIA, whose own ambitions increasingly depended on shaping not only events but perceptions, recognized that foundations offered legitimacy, access, and cover. Through them, the intelligence services could support cultural institutions, university research projects, media ventures, and international organizations without leaving fingerprints that might embarrass the government or expose the operation. And in return, foundations gained insights, connections, and strategic vision that aligned their philanthropic work with geopolitical imperatives.

The relationship was not formalized. It did not require explicit agreements. It arose organically from a shared conviction that the world of the postwar era was too fragile, too interconnected, and too dangerous to be left unmanaged. Both foundations and intelligence agencies believed they were acting in the service of stability, protecting the world from the ideological tumult unleashed by the war and amplified by the rise of the Soviet Union. They saw themselves not as manipulators but as custodians—intellectual guardians of a world that might otherwise slide into chaos.

Yet the convergence of these forces had another effect, one that neither side fully anticipated. It created an ecosystem of influence that operated outside the traditional boundaries of public oversight. Decisions about global health, agricultural development, education, media, and international cooperation were increasingly being devised by a small constellation of institutions whose authority rested not on democratic mandate but on wealth, expertise, and international legitimacy.

And because these institutions acted through grants, partnerships, and cultural initiatives rather than through legislation, their influence was largely invisible to the public. This invisibility made their power more durable, not less.

In the same decade, American media, the great engine of narrative and national identity, was undergoing a transformation of its own. Film studios worked closely with the Pentagon to craft stories that framed American military power as stabilizing and necessary. Radio programs, some openly funded by the State Department, broadcast narratives of freedom and democracy into Europe, Latin America, and Asia. Many magazine and newspaper writers, having worked in wartime propaganda, transferred their wartime perspectives to peacetime journalism, molding public understanding of global affairs through a lens that supported the emerging postwar order.

Television, a new and intimate medium, accelerated this process. Families gathered around screens that delivered not only entertainment but a curated interpretation of the world—one in which the United States appeared as the guardian of global stability, the architect of reconstruction, and the bulwark against chaos. Narratives of international cooperation, humanitarian progress, and scientific advancement flowed through the medium with an ease that made them feel natural, unmanufactured, inherent to the American story.

But beneath the polished surface of these narratives, a more complex truth simmered. The media's role in shaping public understanding was increasingly tied to the imperatives of the National Security State—not through censorship or coercion, but through access, partnership, and influence. Reporters were embedded with military units, given privileged briefings, and invited into the orbit of officials who framed global events in terms that aligned with America's strategic needs. Journalists who challenged these narratives often found themselves marginalized, their access restricted, their stories dismissed as naïve or subversive.

This convergence of foundations, intelligence, and media formed the very architecture of the infiltration of the mind. It did not produce propaganda in the blunt sense. Instead, it produced a worldview, a frame of reference that shaped how Americans understood the world and their place in it. It cultivated a sense of global responsibility that made the expansion of international institutions seem not only necessary but morally imperative.

It fostered a trust in expertise that made the growing power of unelected bodies appear benign. It encouraged a belief in stability over sovereignty, cooperation over independence, technocracy over politics.

And it did so through institutions that the public saw as benevolent, objective, and apolitical.

As the decade advanced, these forces intertwined with the emerging infrastructure of supranational authority. This topic would find its fullest expression in the next chapter, when the United Nations and its constellation of specialized agencies stepped into the global arena with a reach and immunity unprecedented in human history.

But before turning to that architecture, it is important to recognize the magnitude of the shift that was already underway.

For in these years, the architects of the postwar order had discovered something profound:

> **The mind could be the gateway to sovereignty itself.**

The power of influence cannot be understated:

- Influence enough minds, and you influence culture.
- Influence culture, and you influence policy.
- Influence policy, and you redefine the boundaries of a nation.

In this way, the infiltration of the mind was not merely a tool of the Cold War. It was the silent foundation of a new system of governance—one that moved not through conquest or coercion, but through persuasion, narrative, and belief. And the institutions that would embody this system were already taking shape.

–CHAPTER SIX–

FOUNDATIONS OF INFLUENCE

> *"Education is a weapon whose effects depend on who holds it in his hands and at whom it is aimed."*
>
> ATTRIBUTED TO JOSEPH STALIN

IN THE YEARS IMMEDIATELY following the war, as workers cleared rubble from European boulevards and American families settled into the rhythms of peacetime prosperity, another reconstruction was underway—one far less visible but infinitely more enduring. It emerged not from capitals or cabinet rooms but from the boardrooms of philanthropic foundations whose origins preceded the war and whose ambitions far exceeded the boundaries of any single nation. These institutions, created at the turn of the century in the name of public good, had matured into engines of influence capable of shaping the destinies of continents with a subtlety no government could match.

This was not an influence of the brute or coercive variety. It was influence woven through the fabric of thought, through assumptions baked into academic curricula, through research agendas craftily financed, through cultural norms that seemed to arise organically but in truth bore the fingerprints of careful design. The foundations understood something governments often forgot: That the most powerful shifts in history occur not through legislation but through the persistent, yet subtle, redirection of what people consider possible.

By 1945, the Rockefeller Foundation, the Carnegie Endowment, and the newly ascendant Ford Foundation had achieved a kind of intellectual ubiquity. Their names appeared as footnotes to scientific breakthroughs, public health campaigns, economic development plans, and international institutions. But behind the public-facing projects lay a deeper coherence. This shared worldview regarded the nation-state as an impediment to progress and saw world governance as the natural evolution of human society—a new world order, if you will.

This worldview did not emerge spontaneously. It was cultivated across decades, shaped by generations of scholars, industrialists, and diplomats whose own lives had been shaped by global conflicts and who believed that only supranational coordination (i.e., above national coordination) could protect the world from another century of catastrophe.

Yet beneath the idealism lay calculation. Foundations offered something governments could not: *Continuity*. Administrations changed, parliaments dissolved, alliances shifted with the wind. But foundations, governed by trustees whose tenures outlasted presidencies, could sustain a project for decades. They could refine an agenda with the patience of gardeners, planting seeds in academic departments, foreign ministries, and multilateral organizations where they might take root years or even generations later.

It was this continuity that made them indispensable to the emerging global architecture. In the chaotic months after victory, as policymakers struggled to rebuild a shattered world, foundations provided the intellectual scaffolding upon which much of the postwar order was constructed. They offered economic theories to guide reconstruction, legal frameworks for international cooperation, public health models for global management, and educational programs to train the administrators who would manage this new world order.

More importantly, they offered legitimacy. In the eyes of the public, foundations were not political bodies and therefore did not provoke suspicion. They were philanthropic and benevolent. They were intellectual powerhouses. They were concerned only with the betterment of humanity.

This was true—until it was not.

What emerged in the late 1940s was not overt manipulation but a more subtle form of direction, a shaping of the intellectual landscape that would prefigure the political one. Foundations did not issue commands; they issued grants. They did not draft legislation; they financed research that would later justify it. They did not appoint ministers; they funded fellowship programs that produced the men and women who would rise to those positions. And in doing so, they became the architects of the very world they claimed merely to observe.

Their influence, however, was not uniform. The Rockefeller network, with its deep ties to oil, finance, and international diplomacy, exerted a gravitational pull on economic and geopolitical thought. Carnegie, shaped by Andrew Carnegie's belief in peace through intellectual cooperation, focused on law, education, and the creation of global norms. Ford, flush with postwar industrial wealth, became the engine of vast social and cultural programs, ranging from urban redevelopment to psychological research. Each of the foundations operated independently, yet their projects often converged, guided by a shared conviction that the postwar world needed not only rebuilding but redesigning.

This redesign, though meticulously planned, was not without controversy. Critics warned that foundations wielded too much power without democratic accountability, that they effectively operated as shadow governments shaping policy under the veneer of benevolence. But such criticisms rarely reached the public. Foundations were insulated by reputation, by the prestige and wealth of their trustees, and by the absence of any mechanism through which the public could challenge them.

And so, they continued, quietly, methodically, laying the intellectual groundwork for the next stage of the postwar order.

> **The question was not whether the redesign was shaping history. It was how far that shaping would reach.**

Though it would be decades before scholars named it, the postwar years saw the rise of what theorists later called the "epistemic state"—a constellation of institutions that governed not through law but through knowledge. At its center were the great American foundations, which recognized earlier than most that controlling the production and distribution of knowledge meant controlling the horizon of political imagination, will, and policy.

Universities were the first frontier. The war had demonstrated the strategic value of academic expertise—physicists had split the atom, cryptographers had broken the unbreakable, and mathematicians had created new sciences of prediction and control. Foundations understood that universities were not ivory towers but engines of national destiny. And so, they invested heavily, endowing chairs, creating interdisciplinary centers, and financing research that aligned with their globalist vision.

This was not cynicism. Many foundation leaders believed wholeheartedly that humanity had entered an era in which national sovereignty was insufficient to address global challenges. The horrors of the war had convinced them that only cross-border cooperation could prevent another cataclysm. But in their zeal to build this new order, they created an intellectual climate in which certain assumptions became so naturalized that dissenting voices seemed reactionary or even dangerous.

Economic development was a prime example. In the wake of the war, foundations partnered with governments and international agencies to define what development should mean for nations emerging from colonialism or devastation. Their models prioritized industrialization, modernization, and integration into global markets. They funded research on agricultural reform, urban planning, and public administration, each project reinforcing the idea that progress required alignment with Western economic norms. What they did not fund, because they could not imagine it, were studies that questioned the underlying assumptions of this model or that proposed alternative paths rooted in local traditions or political structures.

Thus, development became not a neutral goal but a vector through which foundations extended their influence across the world.

Public health followed a similar trajectory. The Rockefeller Foundation's work in malaria control, yellow fever research, and global health governance set the stage for institutions like the World Health Organization. On its face, this work was unquestionably beneficial. Millions of lives were saved. Yet the deeper impact was less visible: Foundations established the paradigms, the methodologies, and the metrics through which global health was understood. They defined the problems and therefore determined the solutions. And because international agencies adopted these frameworks, the foundations' influence became embedded in the very structure of global governance.

In education, the influence was even more profound. Foundations funded programs that reshaped curricula in schools and universities, promoting internationalism, scientific management, and a vision of citizenship that emphasized global responsibilities over all others. Scholarships sent future leaders across borders, creating networks of influence that spanned continents and ideologies. It was a soft diplomacy more effective than any treaty, cultivating a generation of policymakers who shared a common intellectual language and worldview.

It was in foreign policy, however, that the foundations' influence reached its zenith. The Council on Foreign Relations, long supported by the

Rockefeller and Carnegie funds, became the incubator of American internationalism toward globalism. Its study groups shaped the Marshall Plan, NATO strategy, and the architecture of postwar diplomacy. Journalists, academics, bankers, and diplomats met behind closed doors to debate the shape of the world to come. Presidents listened. Secretaries of State consulted. The public never knew. The architecture of globalism was being formed.

The foundations were not acting in secret; their work was public, their grants published, their trustees celebrated. Yet the cumulative effect of their initiatives created a structure of influence that no government had the power to rival. They built an intellectual world in which policymakers operated, leaving little room for alternatives.

> **This was not conspiracy but consequence.**
> **They had not seized power.**
> **They had cultivated it.**

Europe in the years immediately following the war was a continent suspended between memory and possibility. The magnificent cities of Paris, Berlin, Vienna, and Warsaw carried wounds visible in their damaged exteriors and in their unsettled self-perceptions. Centuries of history had been reduced to rubble. Political systems had collapsed. Economies had imploded. Into this vacuum stepped not only governments but the foundations and private networks that had waited, quietly, for their moment. They saw in Europe's devastation not simply tragedy, but an opportunity to pilot a new kind of reconstruction. It would be one that fused philanthropy, economics, science, and geopolitics into a single, interlocking experiment.

The Marshall Plan, celebrated in American textbooks as modern history's most generous act of national benevolence, was in reality a confluence of political will and private vision. Officially, it was a government program. But in practice, it relied heavily on the intellectual labor, strategic direction, and behind-the-scenes coordination of the same foundations and councils that had guided American internationalism for decades.

Rockefeller-affiliated economists drafted much of the early conceptual framework for European recovery. Carnegie scholars advised on governance reform. Ford Foundation teams embedded themselves in ministries, universities, and research institutes from Rome to Rotterdam. What emerged from this interdisciplinary web was not a simple reconstruction plan but an ideological template: Europe would not simply rebuild; it would be redesigned.

The logic beneath this redesign was as ambitious as it was bold. The nation-state, long seen as the source of both Europe's cultural achievements and its catastrophic wars, was deemed a fragile and potentially dangerous construct. Sovereignty had led to nationalism; nationalism had led to conflict. If Europe was to survive the 20th century, it needed to transcend the very political form that had defined it for centuries. In a sense, nationalism would have to die so that globalism could be born.

Europe would not simply rebuild; it would be redesigned.

Thus, the foundations embraced an idea circulating among intellectuals since the interwar years: *European integration*. What had once been a philosophical musing gained concrete shape in Rockefeller reports, Carnegie policy papers, and Ford-funded research initiatives. Cross-border economic coordination, standardized regulations, shared infrastructure, and supranational institutions were not merely technical solutions but a new architecture of power—one that, if successful, could later be exported to other regions of the world.

And the postwar environment, bleak as it was, proved fertile soil.

France, exhausted by occupation and the collapse of its colonial empire, sought stability at any cost. Germany, divided and disgraced, sought legitimacy through cooperation. The Benelux countries, small and economically intertwined, recognized that unity offered leverage. Together, they embarked on a series of initiatives, including the European Coal and Steel Community, the European Payments Union, and the early steps toward a common market. These reflected not only national interest but the subtle guidance of foundation-funded expertise.

What made this influence so potent was that it appeared natural. Meetings were public. Reports were published. Initiatives were debated. Nothing was hidden, yet everything was shaped, quietly and steadily, by an intellectual vanguard whose loyalties belonged less to any nation than to an idea. The future of governance would not be national but supranational.

This was the European experiment: A controlled demonstration of how foundations could reshape political reality by reshaping the intellectual landscape in which decisions were made. And as integration deepened, it became increasingly clear that this was not merely a European project. It was a prototype—a working model. It was a glimpse into a future in which regional blocs might replace nations, international commissions might override parliaments, and global governance might emerge—not through force, but through a subtle steering toward an over-reaching and comprehensive global goal.

> **If Europe was the proving ground,**
> **then the postwar foundations were its architects.**

But foundations alone could not accomplish such a transformation. They needed institutions through which to channel their influence, and they found the perfect instrument in a body born from the ashes of war: The United Nations.

The creation of the United Nations in 1945 was heralded as a triumph of idealism—the moment when the world declared that diplomacy would triumph over conflict. But beneath the soaring rhetoric lay a more pragmatic truth: The UN was, from its inception, a vessel through which foundations and private networks could extend their influence into the realm of global governance.

The Rockefeller family provided the land for the UN's headquarters—a symbolic gesture that masked a deeper alignment. Their network had been involved in the intellectual groundwork that led to the UN's formation, including early discussions on international law, global health, and economic cooperation. Once established, the UN became a magnet for foundation-funded experts, consultants, and research teams who shaped its programs in ways invisible to the public but undeniable in their impact.

Take UNESCO, the United Nations Educational, Scientific, and Cultural Organization. To most, it was a beacon of cultural preservation and educational reform. But behind the scenes, it was heavily guided by foundations that saw it as the ideal platform for promoting standardized global curricula, scientific cooperation, and the gradual erosion of epistemic boundaries between nations. The Ford Foundation, in particular, poured millions into UNESCO initiatives that aligned with its own vision of modernization and global integration.

Or consider the World Health Organization, whose early programs bore the unmistakable imprint of Rockefeller-funded medical research. From malaria eradication to global epidemiological surveillance, the WHO adopted strategies pioneered in Rockefeller laboratories and field campaigns. With each initiative, the foundation's methodologies became global norms.

Even the economic policy was touched. The UN's Economic and Social Council (ECOSOC), along with its regional commissions, became laboratories for ideas developed within foundation-funded academic circles. Concepts such as development planning, technical assistance, and global statistical systems flowed seamlessly from foundation-sponsored conferences into UN resolutions.

This was not manipulation. It was symbiosis. Foundations provided expertise, funding, and intellectual capital; the UN provided legitimacy, infrastructure, and global reach. Together, they created a new paradigm in which governance increasingly resembled administration—an endless series of technical challenges addressed by experts rather than political questions answered by citizens.

And in this paradigm, the line between influence and authority grew increasingly thin.

But foundations and the UN were only part of the story. To fully understand how power migrated from elected institutions to unelected networks in the decade after the war, one must examine the sphere where secrecy was not a by-product but the operating principle: The world of intelligence.

The war had shown that intelligence was not merely a tool of war but a tool of governance. Signals intelligence had revealed troop movements before battles began. Human networks had penetrated foreign ministries and resistance groups. Psychological operations had reshaped the enemy's morale. The men who directed these operations understood that information, far more than land or armies, was the ultimate currency of power.

After the war, intelligence services did not demobilize. They expanded. They institutionalized. And they aligned themselves, often quietly, with the same foundations and networks that were reshaping the intellectual world.

The Office of Strategic Services (OSS), the precursor to the CIA, had long-standing ties to the academic and philanthropic world—a web of relationships cultivated by men like William "Wild Bill" Donovan and Allen Dulles. William Joseph Donovan did not look like a spymaster. He looked like what he was before he became one: A Wall Street lawyer from Buffalo, broad-shouldered and silver-haired, with the calm authority of a man accustomed to winning arguments in rooms full of powerful people.

He wore his Medal of Honor from the First World War the way he wore everything—quietly, without performance. The decoration was real. So was the man. What made Donovan dangerous was that he understood something most American officials did not: That the twentieth century's decisive battles would be fought not on fields, but in the spaces between institutions. The battles would be fought in the gray zones of intelligence, influence, and covert action where no army could follow.

Donovan had been building toward the OSS his entire career without knowing it. His law practice took him to Europe repeatedly through the 1930s, where he observed the rise of fascism with the trained eye of a man who understood organizational power. He traveled to Spain during the Civil War, to Ethiopia after Mussolini's invasion, to Britain during the Blitz—not as a tourist but as an assessor, filing detailed reports to Franklin Roosevelt on what he saw.

By 1941, when Roosevelt created the Office of the Coordinator of Information and handed it to Donovan, the infrastructure of American intelligence did not yet exist. Donovan built it from scratch, in two years, out of lawyers, academics, journalists, financiers, and adventurers who had never carried a weapon in their lives.

The OSS was Donovan's institution in the deepest sense. He believed intelligence was not a support function for military operations but a strategic instrument in its own right, capable of shaping political outcomes before a single soldier crossed a border. He recruited from the Ivy League and from immigrant communities, from communist sympathizers and conservative bankers, from anyone whose skills could be weaponized for the work. He was not ideological. He was operational.

By 1944, the OSS had operatives in every theater of the war and relationships with every major Allied and neutral intelligence service in Europe. Allen Dulles ran the Bern station from a villa on the Herrengasse, cultivating German industrialists and anti-Nazi contacts with a social ease that owed everything to Donovan's model. James Angleton worked in Rome. Frank Wisner ran operations in Romania.

Truman signed the order disbanding the OSS in September 1945, eighteen days after Japan surrendered. Donovan had lobbied intensively for a permanent peacetime intelligence organization. He was ignored.

The military distrusted him. J. Edgar Hoover lobbied against him. The OSS was dismantled. But dismantling an organization is not the same as dismantling its networks.

The institution died. The people and the methods survived.

When the CIA was established in 1947, the ties between Donovan and Dulles deepened. And the CIA was built on the architecture Donovan had designed, staffed in significant part by people he had trained, and animated by a doctrine—intelligence as strategic instrument, covert action as legitimate statecraft, and secrecy as operational necessity—that was entirely his.

Foundations financed research that fed into CIA analysis. Universities trained analysts who would staff its growing bureaucracy. Think tanks, most notably the Council on Foreign Relations, served as the bridge between intelligence and policy, enabling seamless communication between those who gathered information and those who acted on it.

This alignment was not accidental. It reflected a shared worldview among postwar elites—a belief that stability required the precise management of information, alliances, and economic flows. Intelligence agencies were uniquely positioned to enforce this management across borders, often in ways democratic institutions could not.

But intelligence also served another function: It protected the ideological infrastructure created by foundations. In regions where foundation-funded development programs threatened entrenched power structures, intelligence agencies intervened to preserve the new order. In nations where political movements threatened to reject Western-style modernization, covert operations nudged events toward outcomes favorable to the emerging global architecture.

It was a partnership of necessity, or so they claimed. One with profound consequences.

By the early 1950s, the foundations, universities, intelligence networks, and international institutions had coalesced into something unprecedented: A distributed architecture of influence that operated above the level of national politics yet shaped its outcomes with extraordinary precision.

No single entity controlled this architecture. No conspiracy guided its every move. Instead, it evolved organically from the shared assumptions, relationships, and ambitions of a transnational elite shaped by war, educated in the same institutions, and connected through the same philanthropic and diplomatic networks.

This was not democracy, nor the intended democratic republic. It wasn't even a dictatorship.

It was something new: An epistemic power structure, a soft technocratic order in which political debates unfolded within boundaries set by those who controlled knowledge, funding, and expertise.

Donovan died in 1959, his vision fully institutionalized and his name largely forgotten outside the small world of intelligence professionals who understood what he had made. The CIA erected a statue of him in the lobby of its Langley, VA headquarters. What it cannot convey is the essential quality that made him the founding architect of American covert power: The absolute conviction that the defense of their democracy sometimes required operating entirely beyond its reach.

That conviction outlasted Donovan by decades. It outlasts him still.

For the average citizen, this structure was invisible. They saw the UN as a benevolent institution, foundations as charities, universities as sanctuaries of learning, and intelligence agencies as protectors. They did not see the underlying coherence, the way these institutions reinforced one another's assumptions, the way they converged on a single vision of global governance.

Yet the consequences of this convergence would reverberate through the decades to come, shaping everything from economic development to foreign policy, from education to public health, from media narratives to technological innovation. The foundations of the postwar world had been laid—quietly, durably, and unfortunately to this day, irrevocably.

–CHAPTER SEVEN–

THE UNITED NATIONS AND THE IDEA OF IMMUNITY

"No nation has friends, only interests."

CHARLES DE GAULLE

THE UNITED NATIONS WAS born at a moment when the world seemed desperate for absolution. The ashes of two global wars still choked the air. The ruins of cities still smoldered. Nations staggered through the aftermath like survivors from a shipwreck, clinging to the promise that civilization would never again permit such descent into horror.

When delegates gathered in San Francisco in the spring of 1945, they did so with a mixture of hope, exhaustion, and a kind of solemn determination that comes only after witnessing the very worst of what humanity can do. To the world's public, the United Nations appeared as a cathedral of peace rising from the rubble. It was perceived as a sanctuary in which politics would finally be subordinate to principle, where dialogue would triumph over force, and where humanity could gather under a single roof and commit itself to a more rational age.

But cathedrals have architects, and sanctuaries have design principles that are not always visible to the congregants. The UN's foundations were poured long before the first charter was signed, shaped by private networks, philanthropic dynasties, and wartime alliances that understood, perhaps more clearly than any elected government, that the postwar world would need a new center of gravity. The League of Nations had died because it had clung too tightly to the sovereignty of its members. The new institution would need to transcend sovereignty, not reaffirm it.

Even the land on which the United Nations Headquarters would rise was symbolic. The Rockefeller family's decision to donate the East River site was hailed as an extraordinary gesture of philanthropy. But those who studied the deeper layers of postwar power understood that it represented something else: The formal marriage of private influence and global governance.

It was not just a gift of real estate. It was a declaration that the age of the nation-state was giving way to an era of international administration. The new era would be shaped, guided, and in many ways supervised by the same networks that had shaped the economic and diplomatic landscape of the United States.

The public never questioned this alignment. They saw the gleaming headquarters, the flags fluttering in orderly rows, the blue helmets symbolizing peace, and the General Assembly serving as a global parliament. They believed the institution embodied the purest aspirations of the human spirit. What they did not see, because the design was subtle by intent, was that the UN was built to be something far more complex: A legal sovereign unto itself, endowed with authorities no government had ever possessed, and protected by immunities that removed it almost entirely from oversight.

These immunities, rather than the lofty speeches delivered at its founding, were the real birthright of the UN. They were the invisible architectures that would allow the organization and the constellation of agencies that orbited it to operate across borders, above parliaments, and beyond the reach of national courts. They created a new legal category: Entities that were not nations, not corporations, not bound by constitutions, and yet were empowered to influence the internal affairs of every country on earth.

**This birthright was not an accident.
It was the blueprint.**

The concept of immunity, as old as diplomacy itself, initially served a simple purpose, or so it seemed. The purpose was to protect envoys from the capricious impulses of foreign courts. But in the aftermath of the war, immunity evolved into something far more expansive and unprecedented: A legal shield not for individuals, but for institutions.

The United Nations was granted exemptions so sweeping that they redefined the landscape of international law.

The UN could own property, negotiate treaties, operate banks, transport goods, store records, hire and fire personnel, run field missions, and influence domestic policy. Yet, it was answerable to no electorate, subject to no national jurisdiction. Its documents were inviolable. Its offices could not be searched. Its personnel could not be arrested for crimes committed while on duty. Even its financial transactions existed behind a veil, beyond the scrutiny of any nation that funded it.

What made this architecture so astonishing was how quietly it was adopted. Delegations signed the charter with the jubilant urgency of men eager to leave the past behind, not pausing to consider that they were creating an institution immune from the democratic mechanisms they represented. Newspapers praised the moment as the dawn of a new era. Radio commentators spoke of global unity. Citizens saw hope, not hegemony.

Yet behind the legalese of the UN Charter, a new form of sovereignty emerged—one not derived from land or people but from the absence of accountability. The concept of *international personality*, first drafted by

European legal scholars decades earlier, suddenly found its most powerful expression. The UN was *not*:

- A state. Yet it possessed many of the privileges of statehood.
- A government. Yet it made decisions that governments felt compelled to follow.
- Above the world. It was apart from it, yet it occupied a legal territory unbound by the traditional constraints of nationhood.

Critics, when they raised concerns, were dismissed as cynics or nationalists clinging to outdated paradigms. But history shows a consistent pattern. When institutions acquire immunity, they also acquire the capacity to reshape the surrounding systems without facing consequences for their mistakes, overreaches, or misjudgments. Immunity does not merely protect; it empowers. And empowerment on this scale is rarely surrendered voluntarily.

Immunity does not merely protect; it empowers.

The legal revolution was complete long before the public realized it had occurred.

If the United Nations itself were the cathedral, its specialized agencies were the chambers in which doctrine was crafted, policies were refined, and influence became embedded in the daily lives of nations. UNESCO, WHO, FAO, UNHCR, UNICEF, ILO—the list grew longer each year, each agency bearing its own mandate, personnel, funding streams, and ideological orientation. Yet they all shared one feature: *Immunity*.

This immunity gave rise to a governance structure unlike anything the world had ever seen. Agencies could implement programs inside sovereign states without being subject to those states' legal systems. They could shape educational curricula, public health strategies, labor policies, housing codes, refugee protocols, agricultural standards, environmental regulations, and migration frameworks. And they could do so with the confidence that no lawsuit, no parliamentary inquiry, no presidential decree could compel them to change course.

For many nations, especially those emerging from colonialism or devastation, these agencies were lifelines. UNESCO sent educators; WHO sent doctors; FAO sent agronomists. Diplomatic cables from the era reveal gratitude mixed with dependency. Nations lacking infrastructure or expertise understandably welcomed the help.

But embedded in every program, every mission, every report was a subtle but unmistakable current: The encouragement of global standards, global norms, and global governance.

These agencies did not impose their frameworks.
They embedded them.

The foundations facilitated this embedding. Rockefeller epidemiologists became WHO consultants. Ford-funded educational reformers became UNESCO advisors. Carnegie economists drafted ILO working papers. The networks were fluid, overlapping, and mutually reinforcing. A scholar might pass from a foundation grant to a UN fellowship to a national ministry and back again without noticing the intellectual continuity because it was the water in which he swam. This continuity produced coherence. That coherence produced authority. And that authority produced something even more significant: *Cultural Legitimacy*.

By the mid-1950s, the UN agencies had become the de facto arbiters of modernity. If UNESCO recommended a curriculum model, it was adopted. If the WHO declared a health priority, governments aligned their ministries accordingly. If the ILO published a labor standard, it became the baseline for negotiations.

No vote was taken; no referendum was held. Influence flowed without resistance because it flowed without explicit assertion.

This was not tyranny. It was technocracy wearing the mask of benevolence.

The deeper one examines the structure of UN immunity, the more it becomes clear that immunity was not merely a legal convenience. It was infrastructure. A design principle. The invisible skeleton upon which the entire architecture of internationalism was constructed.

Without immunity, the UN could have been challenged, subpoenaed, investigated, or constrained.

With immunity, it became untouchable. It collected data without disclosing its sources. It operated schools, laboratories, and field offices without revealing internal communications. It negotiated with governments while withholding internal memoranda. It conducted pilot programs that would later shape global policy without ever having to endure the scrutiny that accompanies national experimentation.

> **Immunity permitted innovation.**
> **It also permitted overreach.**

The foundations understood this long before most governments did. Their trustees were well-schooled in corporate law, international finance, and prewar diplomacy. They recognized the strategic value of housing complex, long-term, politically sensitive projects inside an institution that could not be constrained by elections or public opinion. The UN, far from being the enemy of national power, became the instrument through which elites could embed long-term policies without the risk of reversal by future administrations.

This was not conspiracy. It was strategy.

The postwar era had created a paradox: Sovereignty was both sacred and insufficient. Nations refused to surrender authority, but global problems demanded solutions that no single country could enforce. Immunity resolved the paradox by enabling an institution with no army, no territory, and no electorate to wield a kind of authority that no traditional sovereign could match.

It was the perfect tool for a world entering an age of complexity.

To understand the depth of the UN's early influence, one must look not at its resolutions but at the people who animated it. Many were idealists—scholars, economists, doctors, and educators—who believed sincerely in the mission of internationalism. They had seen the horrors of war, the failures of nationalism, and the fragility of human societies. Their dedication was real.

But idealism alone cannot explain the institution they built. Idealism powered it, but structure directed it.

The deeper story lies in the overlap of networks. A Rockefeller epidemiologist might lead a WHO program in Burma, then transition to a university chair funded by Carnegie, then advise a governmental ministry sponsored by Ford. A political scientist specializing in development might draft a UNESCO report, then serve as an advisor to ECOSOC, then publish under a foundation grant. There was no conspiracy; there was simply continuity of worldview.

These individuals were not instructed on what to think. They were selected because of what they already believed. Their commonalities were striking:

- A faith in expertise
- A skepticism of nationalism
- A belief that global challenges demanded global oversight
- An intuition, sometimes articulated, often implicit, that sovereignty must yield when it interferes with the long-term interests of humanity as they see it

This worldview was not imposed from above. It emerged organically from the academic and philanthropic ecosystems that had nurtured them.

The result was a UN that did not need to declare its authority because its authority was exercised through people who acted with an unobtrusive conviction that they were building a better world, one in which crises would be managed by experts rather than politicians, and where humanity's trajectory could be directed rather than merely endured.

Yet for all its achievements, and there were many, the UN's immunized architecture bore consequences that would not become fully visible for decades. Immunity, by shielding the institution from accountability, also shielded it from correction. Mistakes that would have provoked public inquiry in national governments passed unnoticed or unchallenged. Programs that faltered were rebranded, not reformed. Assumptions that proved flawed persisted because no mechanism existed to test them against democratic resistance.

This is the paradox of benevolent authority. It can do great good, but it can also drift without ballast.

By the early 1950s, the drift had begun. No one noticed. They were not meant to.

But as the decades unfolded, it would become increasingly clear that the UN's immunized system, combined with the influence of philanthropic foundations and the rising power of intelligence networks, had created something unprecedented in human history: A governance structure that derived its authority not from the consent of the governed but from the synergy of expertise, immunity, and continuity.

The world was being managed. And the managers were accountable only to themselves.

George Kennan helped design the machinery and knew what he had designed. In February 1946, Kennan, who was then the deputy chief of mission at the U.S. Embassy in Moscow, sent an 8,000-word telegram to the State Department that became the foundational document of American Cold War strategy.

The document, known as "The Long Telegram," argued that the Soviet Union was an expansionist power driven by ideological imperatives that could not be negotiated away. And the United States must adopt a policy of firm containment across every theater where Soviet influence sought to advance. The telegram circulated through Washington's highest levels and was read by James Forrestal, George Marshall, and Harry Truman. Kennan's career was made by it.

Two years later, as the State Department's first director of policy planning, Kennan drafted a recommendation that expanded containment from a diplomatic doctrine to an operational one. Policy Planning Study 23, completed in 1948, proposed the creation of a covert action capability that could influence political events in foreign countries through means short of war—funding non-communist political parties, supporting friendly newspapers and cultural institutions, and cultivating relationships with labor unions and civic organizations. The Office of Policy Coordination, created in response and staffed initially under Frank Wisner, became the operational core of the CIA's covert action program.

By 1950, Kennan was alarmed. The machinery he had advocated for had expanded beyond anything he had envisioned—and was being used for purposes he had not intended. In a memorandum to the Secretary of State, Dean Acheson, that remained classified for decades, he wrote that the covert action program had become "something of a Frankenstein's monster." The program's operators, he argued, had internalized the logic of covert intervention so thoroughly that they no longer asked whether a specific operation was necessary. They asked only whether it was possible. The distinction had ceased to matter.

Kennan resigned from the State Department in 1950. He spent the next five decades as the most eloquent internal critic of the foreign policy establishment he had helped to create. He argued in memoirs, in lectures, and in private correspondence that the United States had built a machinery of intervention whose scale and autonomy had long since outrun any democratic mandate. Kennan was largely ignored by the policymakers who cited his early work while implementing the doctrine he had subsequently repudiated.

He died in 2005 at the age of 101, having outlived the Cold War with the architecture he had drafted and then spent fifty years trying to correct. The Velvet Empire had produced its own most articulate critic. It simply had no mechanism for heeding him. The Velvet Empire of the postwar era was no longer a hypothesis. It was a reality. A new kind of sovereignty—soft, subtle, and supranational—had entered the world. And it would reshape the destiny of nations.

If the idea of *immunity* granted the United Nations a legal shield, the idea of *mandate* granted it purpose. And in the late 1940s and early 1950s, that purpose began expanding with a velocity few anticipated. Mandates were the lifeblood of the new institution. Through them, the UN declared itself competent to address any issue that could be framed as transnational: Health crises, labor disputes, agricultural production, education, culture, family planning, scientific research, and eventually even the environment and global finance.

The sheer scale was staggering, yet it unfolded slyly, almost imperceptibly, like the slow spreading of light across a landscape before dawn. Each mandate seemed reasonable, even noble, on its own. What nation would object to a global effort to eradicate disease? To raise literacy? To preserve cultural heritage? To coordinate labor standards? To manage refugee flows?

The world, exhausted from catastrophe, was eager to believe that good intentions alone could repair the fractures of civilization.

But mandates, once issued, had a habit of expanding.

One of the great lessons of governmental history is that institutions rarely relinquish authority voluntarily. The UN was no exception. With each success, real or perceived, it grew more confident in its ability to shape the internal affairs of nations, often in ways those nations did not fully grasp.

UNESCO began by encouraging the protection of cultural sites. Within a decade, it was issuing policy recommendations on national curricula, literacy programs, and teacher training frameworks that would influence the intellectual development of millions of children. The WHO started with malaria campaigns. Soon, it was defining the acceptable practices of national health ministries, establishing global standards of public health that governments felt obligated to follow. The ILO, one of the oldest international bodies, expanded its reach from labor rights to the broader terrain of economic justice, social protection, and workplace regulation, creating global norms that subtly reshaped national laws.

None of this was portrayed as coercion. It was billed as "cooperation," "coordination," and "technical assistance."

Yet the cumulative effect was unmistakable. The UN agencies became the quiet legislators of a new world order, issuing soft laws—guidelines, frameworks, protocols—that were not formally binding but were treated as such by governments eager to align themselves with international expectations.

Experts today call this phenomenon "*normative power*"—the ability to shape behavior not through force but through the pressure of consensus, reputation, and legitimacy. But at the time, it was something subtler: The emergence of a parallel legal universe, one that existed above the nation-state and increasingly dictated its choices.

And because these norms were produced by organizations enjoying immunity, they could be crafted without public scrutiny, without democratic debate, and without the constraints that were hindering national legislatures.

In the emerging global landscape, the UN did not enforce the law. It *authored* the moral and administrative vocabulary by which nations would govern themselves.

This was not the world the public believed it was entering. But it was the world being built, piece by piece, mandate by mandate.

To understand how the UN had acquired such influence so quickly, one must examine not its public delegates but the private networks that animated its internal life. The foundations—Rockefeller, Ford, and Carnegie—did not merely advise the UN. They staffed it, funded it, and in many cases, architected its programs.

The Rockefeller Foundation's International Health Division supplied the WHO's intellectual blueprint long before the organization was born. Its epidemiologists and public health theorists wrote reports that were later adopted wholesale as UN doctrine. WHO's early malaria and yellow fever campaigns were, in essence, expansions of Rockefeller pilot programs conducted across the tropics during the interwar years.

The Ford Foundation's influence was even more expansive. Its trustees believed that global governance required not just international institutions but a new class of administrators who were modern, secular, scientifically trained, and internationalist in outlook. To that end, Ford financed graduate programs in public administration, development economics, and international relations across Europe, Asia, and Latin America. The students trained in these programs became UN staffers, government ministers, diplomats, development planners—the new managerial class of the postwar world.

Carnegie's influence flowed into the realm of law, education, and peace studies. Its Council on Foreign Relations-linked scholars drafted some of the earliest frameworks for UN peacekeeping, disarmament policy, and international adjudication.

The public saw philanthropy. But behind closed doors, foundation representatives sat on committees, advisory boards, and expert panels. They shaped hiring decisions. They introduced colleagues into key positions. They funded the research cited by UN reports. They shaped the intellectual climate in which UN policies were conceived, justified, and implemented. The historian Inderjeet Parmar later described this structure with precision as an "elite knowledge network." This was a self-reinforcing constellation of experts, institutions, and funders that defined global problems and prescribed global solutions.

To the public, it looked like cooperation. To those inside the system, it felt like destiny.

It is impossible to understand the UN's earliest decades without acknowledging the influence, at times subtle and at times overwhelming, of intelligence agencies. While the UN charter proclaimed it a neutral arbiter of peace, the geopolitical reality of the Cold War transformed it into a battleground where spies moved as freely as diplomats.

The CIA, MI6, and other Western intelligence services recognized early that the UN offered unparalleled access to information, personnel, and influence. Delegates from more than a hundred nations circulated within its halls. Its agencies operated in regions where formal intelligence presence was difficult or prohibited. Its staff enjoyed immunity, protected from national laws and reporting requirements.

This created opportunities.

Declassified files reveal that the OSS, and later the CIA, penetrated the UN almost immediately after its creation. Personnel in the WHO, UNESCO, and the Secretariat occasionally served as informal assets or information conduits. Intelligence officers used diplomatic cover to gather data on foreign governments. Even within the UN's humanitarian missions, field officers sometimes cooperated with intelligence services to track political developments, insurgencies, and foreign influence.

For Western agencies, the United Nations offered something invaluable: Access to the world under a shield that no national authority could lift. For the UN, intelligence services offered something equally useful: Access to information that allowed them to justify expansion of their mandates.

This was not collusion or conspiracy.
It was convergence.

The same logic that guided foundations—the need for global oversight, the belief in technocratic governance, the ambition to shape the postwar world—also guided intelligence agencies, which were tasked with maintaining geopolitical stability.

The UN did not become an intelligence entity. But it became part of the intelligence ecosystem.

This partnership, though muted, gave the UN a kind of situational awareness no previous international body had possessed. It also gave intelligence agencies a moral veneer. The interventions were framed as humanitarian, surveillance was justified as public health monitoring, and political pressure was disguised as development assistance.

The invisible circuitry of the postwar world included:

- An *immunity*, enabling presence
- A *presence*, enabling influence
- An *influence*, enabling control

By the early 1950s, the cumulative effect of these forces—the mandates, the immunities, the foundation networks, the intelligence convergence—began to alter the meaning of sovereignty itself. Nations remained nominally independent. They still held elections, passed laws, and maintained armies. But the context in which they acted had shifted.

Sovereignty no longer meant absolute discretion. It meant operating within a framework of expectations shaped by institutions beyond national control.

A government that ignored UNESCO's educational recommendations risked diplomatic marginalization.

A ministry that resisted the WHO vaccination standards faced global criticism.

A labor department that failed to comply with the ILO conventions risked trade disputes.

A developing nation that rejected development advice from UN agencies risked losing access to loans, technical assistance, and international legitimacy.

This system did not rely on coercion. It relied on consensus—*engineered* consensus.

The UN never declared itself sovereign. It simply acted as if sovereignty were distributed, shared, and conditional. It was an evolving concept rather than an inviolate principle. And because these changes unfolded quietly, embedded within technical programs and expert panels, the public never recognized that the world's political landscape had been fundamentally rearranged.

The decade between 1944 and 1954 was the hinge. It was the moment sovereignty began its transformation from a national inheritance to a managed commodity, overseen by institutions operating above democratic reach.

And the mechanism that enabled this transformation, more than any treaty or charter, was the concept the public understood the least: IMMUNITY.

–CHAPTER EIGHT–

THE VELVET EMPIRE

> *"Every empire tells itself and the world that it is unlike all other empires; that its mission is not to plunder and control but to educate and liberate."*
>
> EDWARD W. SAID

THE MOST ENDURING EMPIRES do not declare themselves at all. They do not unfurl standards from battlements or send armies marching across frontiers. They do not teach schoolchildren to salute a distant monarch or paint maps in the colors of conquest. They work in quieter ways: Through influence disguised as expertise, through authority diffused across institutions, and through structures so elegantly woven into everyday life that their power is mistaken for the natural order of things.

Such was the character of the empire that emerged in the decade following the Second World War—an empire with no capital, no sovereign, and no flag. Its dominion did not lie in territory or tribute, but in the architecture of finance, diplomacy, intelligence, and culture. It was not ruled by a dynasty, but by a constellation of networks whose members shared an education, a worldview, and a conviction that humanity could be guided more effectively by enlightened management than by the unpredictable desires of the governed.

This was "The Velvet Empire."

It did not resemble anything the world had seen. Yet, its contours were unmistakable to those who understood how power migrates from one age to the next. The industrial age had been defined by the visible: Factories, armies, colonial administrations, and maritime trade routes. But the postwar age, the one built between 1944 and 1954, was defined by the invisible: Agreements drafted in private, councils operating without headlines, and economic flows channeled through institutions beyond the reach of national law.

The difference between the Velvet Empire and the empires of the past was not in ambition but in method. Earlier empires imposed themselves upon the world with force. The Velvet Empire entered nations by invitation—legal, financial, and technocratic invitations—to which governments said "Yes" because the alternatives seemed unthinkable. It promised reconstruction, stability, modernization, and expertise. It offered funding, guidance, and coordination. It presented itself as a partner rather than a ruler.

But partnerships that operate through dependence are partnerships in name only.

The architects of this new order understood that sovereignty was not something to be conquered but something to be absorbed, redirected, and managed. Nations would retain their flags and parliaments, their rituals and rhetoric. But the substance of sovereignty—the ability to chart an independent course—would be quietly redistributed across a network of institutions whose origins and obligations did not align with any electorate.

The public did not see this shift. It was not meant to.

They saw prosperity rising, cities rebuilding, a new global apparatus promising peace. They saw the UN, the IMF, the World Bank, NATO, and the Marshall Plan—institutions whose names conveyed order, cooperation, and progress. They saw foundations funding public health campaigns, development projects, and university chairs. They saw intelligence services defending freedom from tyranny. They believed, sincerely, that the world was entering an age in which the worst dangers of the human condition had finally been mastered by reason.

Power often changes form just as it becomes most difficult to recognize.

But power often changes form just as it becomes most difficult to recognize. In the decade after the war, the Velvet Empire crystallized. It took shape not through a single decision but through countless small ones. Treaties were signed in haste, committees were formed to solve temporary problems, advisory groups assembled to offer guidance, and financial arrangements were established to manage crises.

Each decision seemed modest, but together they constructed a supranational architecture capable of guiding nations without ever having to rule them openly. The brilliance of the Velvet Empire lay in its subtlety. Its authority was distributed, not centralized. Its influence flowed through institutions, not individuals. Its power lay in shaping possibilities rather than dictating outcomes.

Where earlier empires imposed, this one curated. Where earlier empires threatened, this one offered assistance. Where earlier empires compelled, this one persuaded, and then insulated itself behind layers of legal immunity to ensure that persuasion would never be challenged.

The stage was set long before the actors recognized their roles.

And no institution embodied this transformation more clearly than the Bank for International Settlements, whose survival through the war had proven the resilience of financial sovereignty when protected by neutrality and shielded by law.

But the BIS was only one pillar. The Velvet Empire's architecture rested on four others: The newly empowered intelligence state, the rise of foundations as global policymakers, the emergence of multinational corporations, and the ascendance of the United Nations as a kind of moral parliament for humanity.

These were not independent developments. They were convergent.

And by the mid-1950s, the convergence had reached its moment of clarity.

> **The world believed it was living in the aftermath of war.**
> **In truth, it was living in the first decade of a new order.**

To understand the Velvet Empire's earliest consolidation, one must return again to Europe—not the Europe of tanks and trenches, but the Europe being reconstructed in conference rooms and planning bureaus. The Marshall Plan is often remembered as the economic miracle that revived a devastated continent.

But beneath the visible story of aid shipments and industrial loans lay another story entirely: The administrative conquest of Europe.

The Plan, as historians like Benn Steil have shown, was designed not only to rebuild economies but to standardize them. Recovery was a pretext for harmonization of currencies, production quotas, trade routes, and ultimately the political expectations of entire nations. The United States did not just send money; it sent administrative logic, delivered through teams of economists, engineers, and policy experts drawn from the very foundations and think tanks that had shaped the wartime and prewar intellectual climate.

Rockefeller economists advised on currency stabilization. Carnegie-affiliated lawyers drafted trade frameworks. Ford-sponsored specialists designed public administration reforms. The Council on Foreign Relations provided the conceptual architecture.

Europe accepted this guidance because it needed it. But acceptance is not the same as autonomy.

The European Coal and Steel Community, hailed as the first step toward integration, was less a triumph of diplomacy than a triumph of administrative thinking. The decision to place Europe's foundational industries under a supranational authority was not merely a symbolic gesture toward peace. It was a structural commitment to a new form of governance, in which national sovereignty ceded ground to regional management.

This was the Velvet Empire in embryonic form. It was an empire built not on domination, but on design. And the designers were not elected officials but experts—economists, administrators, legal scholars, and foundation consultants—whose loyalties were aligned with systems rather than nations.

As Europe moved toward integration, the Velvet Empire found its first willing continent.

But Europe was only one side of the story. The European experiment created the administrative logic, but it was multinational corporations that supplied the momentum. Before the war, corporations had existed within nations even when they operated across borders. After the war, the logic flipped. Corporations operated across borders even when nations attempted to restrain them.

The cause was structural. The postwar recovery depended on scale in energy, transportation, chemicals, and finance.

No single nation could deliver that scale alone. And so, corporations expanded, acquiring subsidiaries, forming alliances, and building global supply chains. This was demonstrated by IBM's expansion into Europe, Lever Brothers' dominance in Africa, and the petroleum giants' reach into the Middle East. Each development chipped away at the practical meaning of borders.

Nations still drew lines on maps. Corporations treated them as administrative inconveniences.

The foundations reinforced this trend, funding management studies, business schools, and academic research that framed multinational expansion as the natural progression of modernity. The UN reinforced it through trade frameworks and development programs. Intelligence agencies reinforced it by protecting corporate interests deemed vital to Western strategy.

> **The Velvet Empire did not need to conquer borders. It simply made them irrelevant.**

Where corporations dissolved borders, intelligence services erected a culture of secrecy. And in doing so, they completed the Velvet Empire's infrastructure.

The CIA, MI6, and their counterparts in Western Europe understood early that information was the new sovereign resource. Nations with access to information could dispense with overt conquest. They could influence outcomes locally and globally through relationships, networks, funding channels, and narrative control.

In Iran, Italy, Greece, Germany, and Japan, the intelligence arm of the Velvet Empire shaped political outcomes not by imposing rulers but by nudging constellations of influence. They did not overthrow the world; they rearranged it. And because their operations were secret, they left no fingerprints—only outcomes.

The public believed their governments acted independently. In reality, national politics had become a stage, and the Velvet Empire wrote and orchestrated the play.

By 1954, the Velvet Empire had achieved something extraordinary: *Coherence*. Coherence across all institutions meant:

- Financial institutions coordinated monetary policy across borders.
- Intelligence agencies coordinated political strategy.

- Foundations coordinated intellectual direction.
- UN agencies coordinated administrative norms.
- Multinational corporations coordinated economic flow.

No single institution ruled. No single leader commanded. Yet the system moved with the unity of a single organism.

This was the most radical transformation of sovereignty since the Peace of Westphalia—and the least understood. Earlier empires were visible. Their ambitions were declared. Their struggles were obvious.

> **The Velvet Empire hid in plain sight, embedded in the architecture of cooperation, diplomacy, and progress.**

Its authority was soft. Its reach was global. Its legitimacy was never contested because its existence was never acknowledged.

But its consequences were profound.

> **Nations appeared to lead. Institutions quietly steered. The public voted. The world was managed.**

And as the decade closed, the Velvet Empire stood fully assembled, awaiting the moment history would reveal its permanence.

If earlier empires were built on the logic of hard power—armies, fleets, colonial administrators—the Velvet Empire advanced through the quiet precision of soft power. This term, coined decades later, inadequately captures the subtlety of what unfolded in the postwar decade. For soft power did not simply attract or persuade; it *structured* the environment in which persuasion occurred. It created the intellectual, moral, and administrative frameworks within which nations made choices, often unaware that the range of choices had already been narrowed.

The postwar foundations played a central role in this transformation. They invested not merely in projects but in paradigms. They promoted modernization theory in universities from Jakarta to Rio de Janeiro. They embedded development economics in ministries across Africa and South Asia. They supported media initiatives that framed Western governance as the inevitable path of progress. They financed scholars, teachers, planners—agents of modernization whose allegiance was not to a nation but to a worldview.

This worldview, articulated by academics like Walt Rostow and later embraced by policymakers in Washington, London, and Bonn, held that societies evolved through predictable stages from tradition to modernity. The role of the West—the role of the Velvet Empire—was to shepherd the world along this path. But modernization theory was not merely descriptive; it was prescriptive. It defined "progress" in ways that aligned with Western strategic and economic interests, and it dismissed alternative trajectories as irrational or dangerous.

Under this intellectual overlay, sovereignty became conditional.

A nation that followed the modernizing script was a partner. A nation that resisted was backward, unstable, even "at risk." This language empowered the Velvet Empire to intervene—politically, economically, and culturally—without appearing imperial.

Intervention was reframed as *assistance.*

Influence was reframed as *partnership.*

> **This sleight of hand defined the postwar world.**
> **It remains the grammar of global governance today.**

As foundations molded thought and the UN guided norms, multinational corporations expressed that reality. They built physical and economic infrastructures that tied nations into systems larger than themselves.

Oil pipelines, telephone networks, chemical plants, shipping routes, and financial exchanges each became a thread in an emerging web.

To those within the web, the connections felt efficient and modern. To those studying the web as a whole, it looked like something else: A lattice of dependence.

Corporations headquartered in New York, London, Zurich, Paris, and Amsterdam did not set out to undermine sovereignty. They simply pursued their interests. But their interests required predictability, evidenced by stable currencies, compliant labor forces, harmonized regulations, and political environments, aligned with long-term investment.

The Velvet Empire provided that stability. In return, corporations reinforced the empire's infrastructure.

By the early 1950s, the world's leading multinationals were indistinguishable from the states that supported them. They contributed to policy through advisory councils. They partnered with foundations on development projects. They cooperated with intelligence agencies to protect supply chains and strategic assets. And they aligned, implicitly and explicitly, with the UN's legal architecture—particularly its immunity frameworks, which insulated their international operations from domestic challenges.

The corporate world did not simply benefit from the Velvet Empire. It became one of its pillars.

None of this would have been possible without the narrative that sustained it. While the institutions of the Velvet Empire were constructing the architecture of global governance, the public was given a different story entirely—a story of peace, progress, and prosperity. The narrative was consistent and convincing:

- Newsreels showed smiling children being vaccinated by the WHO doctors.
- Newspapers printed photographs of UNESCO teachers distributing chalk and textbooks.

- Radio broadcasts celebrated labor reforms crafted with the ILO's guidance.
- Diplomats spoke of "brotherhood," "collective security," and "the family of nations."

These were not illusions. They were genuine achievements. But they were also incomplete. Behind the scenes of every public triumph lay private negotiations, expert committees, legal immunities, and networks of influence operating outside the public's field of vision. The public narrative affirmed that the world was united in moral purpose. The private architecture ensured that this purpose aligned with the strategic interests of the postwar elite and globalists.

The Velvet Empire was not necessarily sustained by secrecy; it was sustained by the illusion of benevolence. People believed in the institutions guiding them because those institutions seemed to address real suffering. They delivered vaccines, built schools, revived economies, and mediated disputes. The moral weight of their accomplishments shielded them from scrutiny.

> **The genius of the Velvet Empire lay in the fact that it made power gentle enough to be embraced and invisible enough to be denied.**

By the early 1950s, the world appeared stable. But stability can be misleading.

Power had not disappeared after the war; it had migrated away from parliaments, electorates, and the visible hierarchies of states. It settled instead in institutions insulated from political turbulence:

- Development banks
- Treaty organizations
- Philanthropic foundations

- Intelligence alliances
- Multinational boardrooms
- Academic councils
- The immunized agencies of the United Nations

This redistribution of power was not necessarily planned by a cabal, nor imposed by force. It emerged through the convergence of ideas, strategies, fears, and ambitions.

But by 1954, the architecture was complete enough to function without its builders. It had become self-sustaining.

A Velvet Empire: Soft in presentation, pervasive in reach, durable in structure, and unanswerable to the public it governed. And in that year, 1954, the empire crossed the threshold from construction to perceived permanence.

–CHAPTER NINE–

1954: PERMANENCE

> *"In the councils of government, we must guard against the acquisition of unwarranted influence, whether sought or unsought…"*
>
> DWIGHT D. EISENHOWER, FAREWELL ADDRESS (1961)

THE OUTWARD CALM OF 1954 was a deception that history would take decades to unravel. To the public, the year appeared almost serene—an interlude in the Cold War, a moment when the economic vigor of the American republic seemed limitless. The horrors of the global conflict felt distant enough to fade into memory. Factories hummed, suburbs sprawled, television sets glowed blue in the windows of new ranch homes, and the American flag seemed to stand at the summit of the postwar world. Yet beneath this smooth surface, 1954 marked the time when the architecture of the emerging international order hardened into something with permanence, something that would subtly direct the destiny of nations long after the generation that built it passed away.

There was a stillness to the year that belied the magnitude of the forces converging behind closed doors. It was as though a curtain had fallen across the public stage, signaling the end of one act and the silent beginning of another. Beneath that curtain, the institutions, networks, and alliances forged in the shadows of war completed their metamorphosis. What had been experimental during the emergencies of the 1940s—the provisional agreements, improvised intelligence partnerships, financial mechanisms designed for reconstruction—solidified into a structure of governance that no electorate had been asked to approve.

It was a structure built not only on policy, but on continuity. Not on treaties alone, but on the belief that certain forms of power must endure, insulated from the vagaries of democratic sentiment.

To understand 1954 is to recognize the culmination of a project that began before the guns of World War II fell silent. The men who had guided wartime diplomacy and postwar reconstruction—Allen Dulles, John Foster Dulles, the Rockefeller networks, the technocrats of Bretton Woods, the industrial councils of Western Europe, the resurrected German corporate class—had all worked with an eye toward a future that required stability above all else. They had lived through the chaos of the 1930s, seen democratic institutions collapse under economic strain, and watched the world descend into ideological barbarism. Their solution was to build a system that could outlast the fragility of electorates, a system that relied on intelligence, finance, and diplomacy, rather than territorial conquest or military force. They believed they were preventing calamity. Most did not understand that they were creating a new form of sovereignty.

By 1954, it was impossible to deny that something irreversible had taken root.

The year began with a paradox. America was at the height of its influence, yet increasingly bound by the very alliances and institutions it had created. The Marshall Plan countries were recovering at breathtaking speed, Germany was reemerging not as a vanquished power but as the industrial heart of Europe, and the multilateral institutions designed to coordinate the postwar economy were now acting with a confidence that suggested not collaboration but direction. The United States, flush with resources and moral authority, found itself tethered to a network of commitments that required its constant participation, its constant subsidy, and its constant leadership, yet offered little room for deviation or retreat.

It was a system that functioned best when the public understood it least.

The CIA, an agency born from wartime necessity and shaped by the clandestine instincts of Allen Dulles, entered 1954 with an unprecedented reach. No longer a fledgling institution unsure of its mandate, the CIA had become a central instrument of American power. Its presence was felt in the corridors of foreign ministries, in the offices of newspaper editors, and in the boardrooms of corporations whose global aspirations dovetailed with America's geopolitical goals.

The agency's actions during this period, whether in Guatemala or Iran, signaled the arrival of a new ethos: The belief that stability justified intervention, and that intervention required secrecy.

Europe, too, was undergoing a transformation that seemed benign on the surface but in fact reflected deep structural ambitions. The European Coal and Steel Community, the precursor to the European Economic Community, was not merely an attempt to bind France and Germany together in peaceful interdependence. It was the opening move in a strategy of integration that dated back to wartime plans drafted by both Allied planners and German industrialists. The Red House legacy, the idea that German economic influence would be resurrected through multinational structures rather than national retaliation, became increasingly visible in the composition of corporate boards, industrial policy councils, and cross-border financial agreements.

And then there was the Bank for International Settlements in Basel. Having survived scandal, wartime controversy, and political scrutiny, the BIS emerged in the early 1950s not weakened but emboldened. Central bankers, recognizing the growing complexity of the global monetary system, treated the BIS not merely as a meeting place but as the quiet anchor of transnational financial coordination. Its immunity from national law, its independence from democratic oversight, and its ability to convene the most powerful financial actors in the world made it the perfect embodiment of the postwar philosophy: Continuity over consent, stability over sovereignty, and discretion above all.

1954 was the year when these independent threads—intelligence, finance, diplomacy, industrial integration—braided themselves into a single fabric.

The public, distracted by prosperity and reassured by the rhetoric of peace, had no reason to suspect that the architecture of global power had shifted from a temporary scaffolding to a permanent structure. But the men at the center of this new architecture knew exactly what they had built. Their conferences, retreats, and informal gatherings were not conspiratorial in the caricatured sense. Yet, they represented an unmistakable alignment: A shared conviction that the world could no longer be entrusted to the chaos of independent nations. A new system—quiet, coordinated, and resilient—was the only safeguard against another descent into disaster.

What they did not anticipate was that this system, once hardened, would prove nearly impossible to reform. And the democratic societies it claimed to protect would eventually feel constrained by its invisible boundaries.

1954 was the hinge. It was the year the curtain dropped. It was the moment when the provisional became permanent.

With that permanence came a new epoch, one in which the world was no longer led by governments alone, but by networks whose authority was derived not from the ballot box but from their own continuity.

The permanence of 1954 did not arrive with declarations or treaties. It arrived with the almost imperceptible shift of institutions slipping quietly into a new posture—no longer provisional, no longer experimental, but confident in their role as custodians of a world that would be managed from above. It is impossible to pinpoint a single meeting or memorandum where this transformation was codified. Instead, it unfolded like the settling of foundations after a house has been built: Silent, steady, and only visible in hindsight to those who know how to look.

In Washington, the posture of the intelligence establishment changed in ways that were subtle but unmistakable. Allen Dulles, after years of maneuvering through the shadows of wartime diplomacy and clandestine negotiations, had finally achieved what he considered the proper architecture for American intelligence. Under his leadership, the CIA ceased to be the cautious newcomer to the world of espionage and instead became its conductor. The agency's successes in Iran and Guatemala in 1953 had emboldened its instincts, convincing its leaders that democracies, left to their own devices, were too fragile to withstand ideological upheaval. Stability, in their view, required intervention, preferably before instability announced itself.

Dulles cultivated an internal culture where covert action was not an extraordinary measure but a routine instrument of policy. His officers spoke a language that blended diplomacy with deception, believing that the American century would collapse if not shepherded through strategic manipulation. They exchanged cables and field reports with the confidence of men who believed the future depended on their discretion, not on the will of the people whose representatives were rarely informed of their operations.

In this environment, secrecy became a virtue, paternalism became a duty, and intervention became a moral imperative.

At the same time, the State Department, under John Foster Dulles, crystallized its own understanding of permanence. Treaties ceased to be occasional instruments of diplomacy and became the steel framework around which entire regions would be bound. Alliances were no longer strategic conveniences; they were commitments into which the United States would anchor itself so deeply that withdrawal was unthinkable. NATO, in particular, became an institution with a gravitational pull so strong that American foreign policy began to orbit around it rather than the other way around.

John Foster Dulles saw alliances as the scaffolding required to keep a fractured world from splintering again. What he did not acknowledge, or perhaps understood too well, was that these alliances also diminished America's ability to act independently of the structures it had birthed.

Across the Atlantic, Europe was quietly rearranging itself into something that earlier generations could scarcely have imagined. The project of reconciliation between France and Germany, while genuine at the political level, was also propelled by deeper forces rooted in industrial strategy and financial integration. The European Coal and Steel Community, conceived as a bulwark against war by tying together the raw materials of conflict, proved far more transformative than its publicly stated purpose. It established the precedent that economic sectors of strategic importance could, and perhaps should, be governed by supranational authority, insulated from the oscillations of national politics.

This was not a theoretical shift. It altered the daily reality of governance.

The ministers and bureaucrats assigned to the ECSC found themselves answering not to their national parliaments but to a European High Authority that operated outside traditional democratic constraints. From this body grew the conceptual seed of a United Europe, one whose decisions would increasingly bypass sovereignty. The logic was simple. Peace required integration, integration required permanence, and permanence required the surrender of certain national prerogatives.

The very language of governance changed, and with it the expectations of future generations.

Behind this public narrative lay a quieter continuation of the Red House legacy. German industrial families who had survived the war—some through collaboration, some through carefully orchestrated reinvention—now guided the reconstruction of their nation with a confidence that suggested continuity rather than rupture. Their companies were reorganized, not dismantled. Their capital networks resurfaced, not confiscated. Their influence expanded under the banner of European rebuilding, not despite it. They entered multinational consortia with ease, drawing on relationships maintained during the war years through neutral intermediaries, sympathetic corporate partners, and the enduring financial channels of Basel.

And Basel itself remained the quiet heart of the new order. The Bank for International Settlements, long the subject of suspicion for its wartime activities, emerged from controversy with a curious advantage: It was indispensable. Central bankers who had once debated its dissolution now admitted, privately, of course, that the world's financial machinery could not function without an institution that lived outside political jurisdictions.

The BIS was not merely a bank; it was a sanctuary for continuity. Policies debated in its conference rooms did not require legislative approval. Their implementation did not depend on elections. The BIS existed in a realm where the abstractions of monetary theory became real, molding the conditions under which national economies operated. Its permanence was guaranteed by its invisibility.

In London, the British establishment, though presiding over the embers of a fading empire, maneuvered deftly to secure a new form of influence. The City of London reconstituted itself as an offshore financial nexus explicitly designed to attract global capital unconstrained by domestic law. British intelligence, still among the most sophisticated networks in the world, deepened its operational compatibility with the CIA and other Western services. Through these mechanisms, Britain retained a form of global reach, not through colonial administration but through financial leverage and covert partnerships.

In a sense, the empire did not disappear; it changed costumes.

The corporate world experienced a similar transformation. Multinational firms, energized by postwar demand and supported by favorable regulatory environments, expanded across borders with unprecedented speed. They were not content to be mere national champions. They envisioned themselves as actors in a global marketplace where regulatory arbitrage, labor mobility, and technological advantage allowed them to transcend the constraints of nations.

Their executives developed an international sensibility, one that aligned naturally with the emerging architecture of global governance. In boardrooms from New York to Zürich, these companies came to view governments not as sovereign authorities but as partners whose policies could be encouraged, influenced, or occasionally circumvented.

In academia and the world of ideas, foundations played a pivotal role in shaping the intellectual contours of the era. Rockefeller, Ford, Carnegie, and their European counterparts funded research programs, academic chairs, international fellowships, and policy institutes that nourished the ideology of integration and global management. The scholars and policymakers cultivated through these programs spoke a common language. It was one that emphasized interdependence, coordination, and the primacy of expertise. They wrote reports, taught courses, drafted policy memos, and advised governments with the steady conviction that the world could only be saved from itself through technocratic oversight.

By 1954, these streams of influence converged, and the architecture hardened.

What distinguished this new order was not its ideology—though it leaned toward internationalism—nor its institutions, though they were powerful. What distinguished it was its permanence.

The structures built during the previous decade became the unspoken assumptions of governance. They were no longer experiments; they were the environment. They framed the choices available to leaders. Nations were tied to unalterable agreements. The public consumed narratives that they shaped. Their influence determined who gained power and what policies were viable.

The permanence of 1954 was not imposed through force. It was accepted through familiarity. It whispered itself into existence.

And once it did, the world that had existed before the war—the world of independent sovereignties, mutable alliances, and national primacy—became something like a memory, a shadow of an earlier age.

1954 was the year the new order declared itself, without ever needing to speak.

There was something strangely tranquil about the American imagination in 1954, a kind of soft certainty that the world had settled into its final shape. It was the year when television fully supplanted the radio as the hearth of the modern home; when the suburban streets of Levittown and its imitators became the emblem of a nation that believed it had earned its rest. Eisenhower's calm demeanor reassured a citizenry that had endured two decades of upheaval.

The Korean War's ceasefire, however uneasy, allowed families to believe the bloodletting of the twentieth century might finally be ebbing. The very texture of daily life—the chrome curves of automobiles, the scent of fresh-cut lawns, the jingle of neighborhood children riding Schwinn bicycles until dusk—seemed to whisper that the future would be orderly, prosperous, and secure.

Yet that serenity was a mirage, a projection reflected back at the public by institutions that had discovered the power of narrative at the very moment they learned how to operate behind it. The postwar world had not grown simpler. It had grown more organized—meticulously, architecturally, almost mathematically—by networks of influence whose inner workings were inscrutable to all but those seated at the highest tables of power.

This was the paradox of 1954: The more seamless the world appeared, the more intricate its machinery became. And the more intricate its machinery became, the less visible it was to the people whose lives it shaped.

Washington mastered this paradox with remarkable skill. Eisenhower's quiet confidence, his emphasis on moderation, and his genial dismissal of ideological extremes all gave the impression of a government settled into responsible stewardship. His administration projected a fatherly calm, the same poised restraint he had displayed on the battlefields of Europe. The public saw him as the embodiment of a nation stepping into middle age, confident enough to relax its shoulders without entirely forgetting its duties. Yet beneath that veneer of placid governance, the machinery of the National Security State operated with a precision and autonomy that no previous president had commanded or fully understood.

The more seamless the world appeared, the more intricate its machinery became.

The CIA, having tasted decisive influence abroad, now sought to refine its methods into a doctrine. Its assessments shaped foreign policy more thoroughly than State Department cables or diplomatic briefs. Its covert actions, once debated cautiously, became integrated into strategic thinking. It was no longer an agency responding to crises; it had become an agency that pre-empted them, sculpting realities before they could take form. The plausible deniability that shielded its operations was not merely legal protection; it was an ethos, a worldview predicated on the belief that truth was a luxury the Republic could not always afford.

Congress, for its part, had neither the access nor the appetite to scrutinize this evolution. Oversight committees received only what the intelligence community chose to reveal, and even then, the disclosures were framed in language so elliptical, so sanitized, that genuine understanding became elusive. The very people responsible for guarding the Republic found themselves navigating a maze of euphemisms, briefings without detail, and policies presented as "faits accomplis."

The public assumed their representatives were *informed*.
Their representatives assumed the experts were *truthful*.

In the space between those assumptions, secrecy grew like ivy along the façade of the Capitol.

Meanwhile, the public narrative of the Cold War served as a stabilizing force. The threat of communism—genuine in many places, exaggerated in others—provided the perfect justification for the expansion of invisible authority. Americans believed they were participating in a grand struggle between freedom and tyranny. They did not see the degree to which the struggle required, or purportedly required, the consolidation of power into structures that operated beyond their reach.

The nation rallied around symbols: The flag raised over foreign bases, the stern warnings issued by cabinet secretaries, and the patriotic fervor of newsreels and evening broadcasts. These symbols offered comfort, even pride. But they also disguised the deeper transformation that America's strength no longer derived solely from its democratic institutions, but increasingly from its intelligence apparatus, its economic leverage, and its alliances with institutions that had no electoral mandates.

In Europe, the public illusion was even more pronounced. Newspapers celebrated cooperation between nations that had once been bitter enemies. Coal and steel flowed across borders under the new supranational framework, and politicians hailed the progress as proof that the horrors of the past would never return.

Yet beneath these optimistic tones, the true engine of integration operated quietly in conference rooms occupied by industrial magnates, central bankers, and administrators groomed by foundations that spoke the language of global interdependence. Ordinary citizens saw the benefits—rebuilt cities, restored employment, rising standards of living—but they did not see how decisions that once would have been debated in national parliaments were now crafted in multinational councils, where the voices of voters were faint at best.

Germany's resurrection was the clearest example of this dissonance. The public narrative framed it as a triumph of Western generosity, a restoration rooted in shared values and mutual necessity. But those who looked more closely—the few historians, journalists, and dissidents who dared to question the official story—recognized the unmistakable footprints of the industrial dynasties that had met in Strasbourg at the Maison Rouge. The companies that dominated the German "economic miracle" were the heirs of firms that had operated through the war with ruthless efficiency and had survived the Reich by dispersing assets through Swiss banks, Argentine subsidiaries, and friendly corporate alliances. Their return to prominence was not a fluke. It was the fruition of a continuity plan conceived long before Berlin fell.

The same pattern emerged across institutions that mediated global governance. At the United Nations, the broad public emphasis on peacekeeping and cooperation obscured the steady accumulation of bureaucratic authority within its specialized agencies. The World Health Organization expanded into realms once considered sovereign responsibilities. UNESCO shaped educational norms across continents. The International Labour Organization (ILO) influenced domestic labor standards far more than most national unions.

These agencies, protected by legal immunities enshrined in international agreements, operated with a freedom unavailable to any domestic institution. Their reports were treated as objective truths, their recommendations as moral imperatives. Few citizens understood the extent to which these agencies were intertwined with the foundation networks that financed not only their programs but the intellectual frameworks that justified their expansion.

This dynamic, the public illusion of democratic continuity and the private reality of technocratic consolidation, defined the year more profoundly than any single event or policy shift. It created a world in which the familiar architecture of national sovereignty still stood, but the authority it represented was increasingly symbolic.

Governments continued to hold elections, draft budgets, and legislate on domestic issues, but the parameters of their decisions were shaped by institutions that existed beyond their jurisdiction. Central banks coordinated through Basel. Intelligence services coordinated through shadow channels that no constitution acknowledged. Supranational agencies drafted frameworks that domestic policymakers incorporated as though they were inevitabilities.

And all the while, the public believed itself to be living in an age of unprecedented transparency and peace.

It was this disjunction, this widening gap between what citizens perceived and what the architects of the postwar order practiced, that imbued 1954 with its lasting significance. For the first time in modern history, the world entered a period in which systems of power did not merely operate behind the scenes; they operated in a separate dimension entirely, a realm where legitimacy flowed from continuity rather than consent, from coordination rather than representation.

> **1954 was not the year the world was *lost*.**
> **It was the year the world was *hidden*.**

The most striking truth about 1954 is that nothing monumental appeared to happen. The year passed without the cataclysms that defined the decades before it: No global war, no financial crash, and no dramatic shift in borders or ideology. It was precisely this quietness, this absence of spectacle, that allowed the consolidation of the postwar order to proceed without scrutiny. The world had grown accustomed to great upheavals. In the silence that followed, its architects built the infrastructure of a global system meant to render upheaval obsolete.

The consolidation was not announced but discerned only in retrospect through subtle realignments whose significance seemed slight at the time. It occurred in the dark corners of ministerial meetings, in correspondence between central bankers who preferred to leave no paper trail, in the internal memoranda of foundations that spoke of "coordination," "standardization," and "international best practices." All terms that appeared benign but carried within them the beginnings of a new political grammar.

Nowhere was this consolidation more palpable than in the realm of finance. In the early months of 1954, the governors of the leading central banks convened in Basel with a regularity that startled even their own deputies. The Bank for International Settlements had become more than a forum; it had become the de facto sanctuary of global monetary governance. The governors arrived without fanfare, leaving no public record of their agenda. In those unadorned conference rooms, they drafted the principles that would soon guide the stabilizing mechanisms of Western currencies—decisions that would later be presented to national governments as technical necessities rather than political acts.

These meetings revealed something essential about the emerging world. Monetary governance was no longer an expression of national will but an act of transnational stewardship. The men who shaped currency policy regarded themselves not as representatives of sovereign nations but as custodians of a fragile system whose survival required discretion. They believed that if the public understood the precariousness of global finance, or the extent to which the decisions affecting their livelihoods were made by people they had not elected, the entire architecture might collapse.

In their minds, secrecy was not subversion.
It was prudence.

Europe's reconstruction deepened this trend. As the year unfolded, industrial coordination across the continent reached a level of integration that surprised even the original advocates of cooperation. The European Coal and Steel Community, initially conceived as a measure to prevent war, became the experimental framework for broader economic unification. Yet, beneath the technocratic language of integration lay a continuity of influence that traced back to the darkest chapters of the previous decade.

German industrial combines, once at the heart of the war machine, now positioned themselves as indispensable pillars of a peaceful Europe. Their directors, many of whom had evaded meaningful accountability, moved effortlessly through the corridors of the new European institutions, offering expertise that bureaucrats were only too eager to accept.

It was in this convergence of old networks with new governance structures that the true consolidation occurred.

The Red House legacy—the plan drafted in Strasbourg as the Reich crumbled—did not manifest as a rebirth of authoritarianism. Instead, it re-emerged as a subtle but unmistakable presence in the skeleton of the continental economy. German firms reconstituted themselves under new legal forms, expanding their reach through mergers, investment partnerships, and cross-border supply chains. They were no longer the instruments of a regime. They were the engines of a system that valued efficiency and continuity above all else.

Parallel to this economic consolidation was the subtle expansion of the intelligence world. The CIA, emboldened by recent successes, entered 1954 with a sense of mission that bordered on inevitability. It viewed global influence not as a privilege but as an obligation. Its officers, trained in the methods of wartime clandestinity, transferred those skills seamlessly into the geopolitics of the new era.

They moved through embassies, foreign ministries, and corporate offices with a confidence derived from the belief that they were safeguarding the free world. Their growing influence was justified by the dangers they claimed to perceive: Communist infiltration, political instability, and the spread of ideas that threatened the delicate balance they believed they had been entrusted to maintain.

In truth, the dangers were real, but the authority assumed in combating them grew without limit. This expansion occurred not through dramatic declarations but through incremental adjustments: A new liaison desk here, an expanded intelligence-sharing agreement there, and a covert operation undertaken with the tacit consent of allies who preferred to outsource their more unsavory responsibilities.

The invisible state, once justified by wartime necessity, now justified itself by the permanence of the Cold War.

It was an institution that grew to fill every space it inhabited. By 1954, it had woven itself into the very fabric of Western governance.

On the diplomatic front, Washington's web of alliances reached a level of maturity that further entrenched the new order. NATO, only five years old, evolved from a defensive pact into a structure for political and military synchronization on a level never before attempted. American policymakers viewed the alliance as indispensable, not only for European security but for global stability. The rhetoric was that of cooperation.

The reality was that NATO created a system of dependency. Europe relied on American military strength, and the United States relied on Europe's acquiescence to its strategic vision. These interlocking needs created a bond that was stronger than treaty language could express. It was a bond that rendered sovereignty increasingly conditional.

The United Nations deepened its own consolidation almost invisibly. Its agencies expanded their mandates into fields previously considered exclusively domestic: Health, education, labor standards, and agricultural development.

Their reports became benchmarks for nations seeking legitimacy. Their programs influenced national budgets. And their standards shaped the curricula of schools, the regulations of workplaces, and the policies of ministries.

Because these agencies operated behind the shield of international immunity, their influence grew without the friction of public dissent. They existed in a realm where power was exercised through expertise, not representation—a realm that distinguished itself from the democratic traditions of the nations whose flags hung outside the UN building.

Meanwhile, foundations operated as the intellectual armature of the new world. They funded academic programs that taught the virtues of integration. They supported scholars whose work reinforced the necessity of global coordination. They established fellowships that trained future leaders to think in terms of systems rather than nations.

Through conferences, publications, and grants, these foundations created a consensus that the future belonged not to sovereign peoples but to institutions capable of transcending them. It was a soft consensus, but one with profound implications.

In this way, 1954 became the fulcrum of the age. It was not a year of upheaval, but a year of alignment. All the streams of influence that had been flowing separately—the intelligence networks, the financial mechanisms, the industrial alliances, the diplomatic architectures, the supranational agencies, and the philanthropic cadres—converged into a single river. It flowed quietly, steadily, beneath the surface of public life, creating a current that would carry the world into the final decades of the twentieth century.

The unseen consolidation of 1954 did not require the consent of nations. It required only their participation.

And by the time anyone realized what had happened, the new order had taken root so deeply that it no longer appeared new at all. It appeared inevitable. That inevitability was the true hallmark of permanence.

There comes a moment in the life of every political system when the forms of a representative government remain in place, but their substance begins to fade. It does not happen with coups or crackdowns. Instead, it happens through a slow sedimentation of decisions made outside the realm of public understanding—each one small enough to escape notice, but cumulative enough to reshape the nature of authority.

By 1954, the Western world had entered precisely such a moment. Nations continued to hold elections, legislatures continued to debate budgets, and presidents continued to appeal to the people. Yet the true center of gravity had shifted elsewhere, to a realm where permission was no longer required because the mechanisms of governance had moved beyond the jurisdiction of voters.

The transformation was not a conspiracy in the dramatic sense. It was the logical outcome of a decade spent navigating the complexities of postwar reconstruction, geopolitical rivalry, and economic interdependence. The world's most powerful institutions—the central banks, the intelligence agencies, the multinational corporations, the supranational agencies of the United Nations, and the transatlantic alliances—had grown used to acting with speed and discretion. They had learned that public scrutiny slowed their work and that political debates jeopardized the delicate balances they managed.

The notion that policy should be shaped by expertise rather than popular will became an article of faith in these circles, cemented by the belief that the dangers of the modern age required a level of coordination that democratic processes could not reliably provide.

As a result, more and more decisions were made before governments even realized they were no longer in control of the variables. Interest rates were coordinated in Basel long before national legislatures received briefings about inflation. Intelligence operations altered the political trajectory of nations years before their citizens understood the forces shaping their futures. Corporate mergers and cross-border investments reorganized the world's industrial landscape without passing through any democratic filter.

The most consequential policies affecting everyday life, from currency valuation to geopolitical alignments, were crafted in rooms without microphones, recorded only in the memories of the men who attended. And the public, sheltered within the optimism of the 1950s, continued to assume that the nation-state remained the fulcrum of authority. They believed:

- Presidents directed foreign policy.

- Congress shaped economic priorities.
- The people, through the ritual of elections, determined the direction of the Republic.

These beliefs were sincere, rooted in the traditions of the American experience. But they were increasingly out of sync with the world being constructed beneath the surface of their daily lives.

In many ways, the year 1954 marked the dawn of a paradox. The stronger the institutions of global coordination became, the weaker the visible mechanisms of national sovereignty appeared. This was evident not only in the United States but across Europe, where governments found themselves constrained by commitments that limited their autonomy even as they touted the benefits of integration. France could not set certain trade policies without disrupting the carefully balanced arrangements of the Coal and Steel Community. West Germany, newly rehabilitated and eager to assert itself, nonetheless found its fiscal policies quietly shaped by the expectations of international financial institutions. Italy and the Benelux countries discovered that their industrial strategies were now entwined with decisions made in foreign capitals and multinational boards.

Nothing demonstrated this shift more acutely than the evolution of intelligence cooperation. What had begun as a wartime necessity—the pooling of Allied intelligence assets to defeat the Axis—had evolved into a permanent, transnational apparatus. The "Five Eyes" network, though still in its infancy, had already created an intelligence sphere that transcended the authority of any individual government. The Five Eyes encompassed Britain, the United States, Canada, Australia, and New Zealand. They shared intercepted communications, code-breaking capacities, and espionage capabilities as though they were departments of the same unseen ministry. Each nation participated, but none fully governed the network. It existed above them, an entity whose logic and methods belonged to a new era.

The United States held the lion's share of operational capacity, but even Washington found itself increasingly bound by the commitments of global intelligence coordination. Once surveillance, along with covert action, became internationalized, it grew beyond any single nation's ability to restrain. In this context, 1954 was the year the invisible state ceased to be an instrument of policy and became instead the scaffolding upon which policy itself was built.

The same pattern unfolded in the world of finance. The Bretton Woods System, now fully operational, created an international monetary structure that limited the flexibility of national governments while granting unprecedented authority to central bankers. Fixed exchange rates, capital controls, and IMF consultation requirements turned monetary policy into a shared enterprise, where the preferences of one nation could not diverge too sharply from the expectations of the whole.

Countries that attempted to break free found themselves facing currency crises, capital flight, or diplomatic pressure. As a result, the sovereignty they exercised was bounded by invisible constraints—constraints understood intimately by the architects of the system but rarely acknowledged in the rhetoric of political leaders.

Perhaps the most remarkable feature of this new order was how seamlessly it integrated the corporate world into its structure. Multinational companies became informal partners in the governance of economic life, negotiating directly with governments and international institutions. Their decisions about production, supply chains, research, investments, and market expansion shaped the economic realities of entire regions. They operated across borders with a level of fluidity that nation-states could not match, and in doing so, they effectively rewrote the meaning of economic sovereignty.

By 1954, the world had not abandoned the concept of democracy. It had simply outgrown the version of democracy that presumed nations acted independently of one another. What replaced it was a hybrid model—a world governed by elected officials in form but managed in practice by networks whose authority derived from expertise, continuity, and discretion.

These networks rarely seemed to act with malicious intent. Many of their members sincerely believed they were protecting the world from chaos, from ideology, from instability. But sincerity did not alter the fact that they operated beyond public view, accountable only to themselves and to the logic of the systems they had built.

In this sense, 1954 stands as one of the quietest revolutions in modern history. The old world of sovereign nations did not collapse. It simply dissolved into a new arrangement—one in which the levers of power were no longer pulled by those the public could see.

In the silence of that year, a new world order assumed its lasting form—a world that did not ask permission because it no longer needed to.

By the last months of 1954, the transformation that had been unfolding across the decade was complete, though almost no one outside the highest levels of government, finance, industry, and intelligence understood the shift. The world had entered a new configuration so gradually, so quietly, that it lacked the drama historians typically associate with epochs. There was no Versailles Treaty announcing its arrival, no Yalta Conference mapping its contours, no victory parade marking its domination. Instead, it drifted into place like the tide. Slow, certain, and unnoticed until the shore had changed.

The United States entered the year believing it was the steward of the free world. By the end of the year, it had become something more complicated—an anchor within a system whose needs increasingly defined its choices. To preserve the stability of Western Europe, to maintain the Bretton Woods financial order, to keep a fragile peace in

Asia, to guard against the encroachment of Soviet influence, Washington accepted constraints it did not articulate publicly and perhaps did not fully recognize privately. The nation had envisioned itself as the architect of a stable international order; it had not quite realized that the architecture would bind the builder as firmly as it bound the world.

Eisenhower sensed the shift in ways he never openly confessed. A general who had once commanded armies across a continent now presided over a government whose most significant operations occurred in the shadows, beyond his direct view. The intelligence briefings he received were confident and concise, but beneath their polished summaries lay webs of relationships and operations that eluded even his comprehension. The sprawling security apparatus that had emerged from the turmoil of World War II had matured into something self-propelling, something that interpreted his directives in ways that expanded its mandate rather than constrained it.

Eisenhower, cautious by temperament, understood the paradox. The peace he cherished required a machinery that threatened the very republican values he had sworn to uphold.

In Europe, the political classes embraced integration with a mixture of relief and resignation. The horrors of the war were still fresh; the ruins had barely disappeared beneath new construction. For many leaders, the idea of pooling sovereignty seemed a small price to pay for the promise of stability. Yet the public rhetoric of unity masked a deeper truth.

The first supranational institutions were designed not merely to prevent war, but to limit the capacity of democratic electorates to disrupt the fragile balance of recovery.

Their founding documents spoke of cooperation.

Their administrative structures reflected something closer to technocratic guardianship.

In Germany, whose rebirth astonished the world, the year marked a return not merely to prosperity but to influence. The very networks that had convened at the Maison Rouge a decade earlier now re-emerged in sanitized form, directing industrial growth from behind the neutral shield of multinational partnerships. The Wirtschaftswunder (also known as the "Miracle on the Rhine") was real.

Still, its underpinnings lay in the continuity of industrial expertise, capital networks, and managerial cadres that had survived the fall of the Reich intact. Their power was no longer ideological. It was structural, hidden in the flows of steel, chemicals, machinery, and investment capital that sustained the continent.

And through it all, the Bank for International Settlements continued to operate as the quiet hinge of the emerging order. Its conference rooms hosted discussions that shaped interest rates, currency flows, and credit conditions for an entire hemisphere. Its status as an extraterritorial institution allowed it to function without interruption or oversight. The decisions made in Basel influenced the lives of millions who had never heard its name. The bank did not seek publicity; it sought continuity. And continuity, by 1954, had become the lodestar of the new world.

In this context, the United Nations, along with its proliferating agencies, assumed a role that would define the second half of the century: The institutionalization of global norms. Though still in their infancy, bodies like UNESCO, the WHO, and the FAO expanded their footprint into areas traditionally understood as sovereign prerogatives.

They issued guidelines that soon became de facto regulations. They crafted standards that governments adopted. Not because they were compelled to, but because refusing them seemed archaic, parochial, or even irresponsible.

> **The genius of the system lay in its subtlety:**
> **Soft law that behaved like hard authority.**

By year's end, a remarkable inversion had occurred. Where once nations had defined the parameters of international cooperation, now the international system defined the parameters within which nations could operate. The change was quiet but profound, like the slow turning of a ship whose passengers notice nothing until the coastline has vanished behind them.

> **What made 1954 the hinge of the age was not any single institution or policy. It was the convergence of all these forces into a self-reinforcing whole.**

Intelligence alliances ensured geopolitical stability. Financial coordination ensured economic consistency. Corporate integration ensured industrial interdependence. Supranational agencies ensured the diffusion of global norms. And foundations ensured that the intellectual class embraced the logic of the system before anyone thought to question it.

By the time the public began to sense that something intangible had shifted, the architecture of permanence had already set like concrete.

The genius, and the danger, of this new order was that it did not need to declare itself. It did not need constitutions or manifestos. It did not need the consent of the governed in any formal sense. It needed only inertia, expertise, cooperation among elites, and a world that was weary of destruction.

In that exhaustion, the custodians of stability found their opportunity.

They built a system that promised peace, prosperity, and order. They succeeded in ways the nineteenth century could never have dreamed. But in the process, they altered the nature of freedom, sovereignty, and democratic agency in ways the twentieth century struggled to understand.

This was the legacy of 1954:

- A world whose governing logic no longer resided in its nations, but in the silent networks that transcended them

- A world whose permanence was both its greatest strength and its most perilous illusion

For once, permanence is mistaken for destiny, the possibility of renewal becomes harder to imagine, and the structures built to preserve peace begin, slowly and silently, to define the limits of freedom.

–CHAPTER TEN–

A WORLD MANAGED

> *"The whole aim of practical politics is to keep the populace alarmed and hence clamorous to be led to safety."*
>
> H. L. MENCKEN

THE TRIALS THAT OPENED in Nuremberg in November 1945 were, by any measure, an extraordinary achievement. For the first time in history, the victors of a global war had chosen prosecution over summary execution and had insisted that even the architects of industrial genocide deserved due process before judgment was rendered. The moral ambition was genuine. So was the legal innovation. The Nuremberg Charter established individual criminal responsibility for crimes against humanity, created the concept of aggressive war as an international crime, and laid the jurisprudential foundation for every international tribunal that followed.

What it did *not* do was dismantle the networks.

Of the twenty-four defendants in the main trial, twelve were sentenced to death. Seven received prison terms. Three were acquitted. The proceedings generated ninety volumes of documentary evidence and established a historical record of Nazi criminality that remains definitive. By any conventional measure of postwar justice, Nuremberg succeeded. But Nuremberg was one trial. The networks were everywhere.

The subsequent proceedings, twelve separate trials of doctors, judges, military commanders, and industrialists conducted between 1946 and 1949, told a more complicated story. The industrialists' trials revealed the depth of corporate entanglement with the Reich. IG Farben executives who had directed the construction and operation of a synthetic rubber plant at Auschwitz, built and staffed with slave labor, received sentences ranging from eighteen months to eight years. Most were released early.

By 1951, John J. McCloy, exercising his authority as U.S. High Commissioner for Germany, had commuted or reduced the sentences of a significant number of convicted war criminals—industrialists, generals, and SS officers among them—on grounds that ranged from poor health to the demands of West German reintegration.

The message, heard clearly by those paying attention, was that the postwar order had limits on how far it was willing to pursue accountability when accountability conflicted with utility. What Nuremberg produced was a partial reckoning—monumental in its documentation of atrocity, limited in its disruption of power. It told the world what had happened. It did not fully dismantle the machinery that had made it possible.

The trials ended. The networks continued.

History recorded the verdicts. It paid less attention to the commutations, the early releases, the quiet rehabilitations, and the boardroom returns that followed. That part of the story did not fit the narrative of justice triumphant. Instead, it fit the story of infiltration.

Five years after Nuremberg, the system that those same networks had helped build faced its first operational test. The world that emerged in the early 1950s bore a polished veneer that seemed almost designed to soothe. Newspapers announced record growth, new home starts, and surging consumer confidence. Television, still young but rapidly colonizing living rooms, projected a sense of order that felt like destiny itself. Suburbs unfurled beyond city limits like modern American hedgerows. Whole towns sprang from farmland in precise grids—Levittowns of optimism, each house broadcasting the same message. Security had returned.

Yet if one could peel back the surface of those years and step into the corridors that carried the hum beneath the hum, a different portrait would reveal itself. The true architecture of the postwar era was not resting in the Oval Office, nor in Congress, nor in the freshly formed NATO command posts.

It rested in systems—in committees, councils, financial boards, intelligence partnerships, and international institutions—whose reach was expanding quietly, relentlessly, and without the public ever fully realizing what had been fashioned in its name.

The Cold War, with its stark moral lines and cinematic tension, obscured a subtler transformation. Governments were becoming fewer centers of decision and more conduits in a vast managerial apparatus designed to maintain global equilibrium. Policy moved gradually out of the arena of democratic contest and into the shadow of expertise. It was a word that in this era expanded to encompass everything from nuclear strategy to agricultural quotas, from currency stabilization to psychological operations.

The United States, flush with victory and convinced of its global mission, drifted almost unknowingly into this managerial posture. To preserve peace, alliances needed to be strengthened. To strengthen alliances, intelligence had to flow. To manage intelligence, new agencies had to expand. To sustain economies, international financial coordination was required.

And with every step, the world grew less dependent on national judgments and more dependent on the calculus of institutions that did not stand for election, did not respond to constituencies, and did not consider themselves temporary instruments.

What looked like a stable postwar world was, in fact, a world being administered—and increasingly administered from above.

The shift had begun in the last months of the war. But by 1954, it had hardened into permanence. The decade that had begun with rubble and sacrifice now crystallized into a kind of polished inevitability. The public believed the nation was returning to the world the founders had envisioned.

But in truth, the nation was gliding deeper into a structure the Founders could never have imagined—a world not governed but managed. And the managers were no longer in the background. They were the system.

The new managerial class did not announce itself with the bravado of politicians. Its influence was expressed instead in decisions that seemed technical, administrative, or logistical. These were the sort of decisions the average citizen rarely noticed because they came wrapped in the language of necessity.

These managers were the heirs of the war's strategic class: The men who had run supply chains across oceans, who had coordinated intelligence with allies, who had planned invasions that required mathematical precision and bureaucratic obedience. In wartime, such coordination was indispensable. In peacetime, it became a model.

Alan Dulles embodied this transformation, bridging effortlessly between wartime espionage and postwar governance. The silent confidence he projected—part lawyerly detachment, part aristocratic certainty—reflected something deeper than personal charisma. It reflected an entire worldview carried by the managerial elite: The belief that the world was too complex to leave in the hands of elected officials who came and went with the unpredictable rhythm of democratic will.

Dulles's CIA became not merely an intelligence agency but a kind of global crisis management apparatus, tasked with preserving stability wherever disorder threatened. Its operations stretched from the jungles of Southeast Asia to the deserts of the Middle East, from the corridors of European parliaments to the presidential palaces of Latin America. Each intervention was framed as a protection against Soviet expansion, but beneath that justification was another truth. The agency was assuming responsibility for outcomes once left to sovereign governments.

Meanwhile, the State Department, especially under John Foster Dulles, evolved into a diplomatic organism whose first loyalty was not to the shifting tides of American public sentiment but to the overarching stability of the international system itself. Treaties multiplied, commitments deepened, and the idea of America as a sovereign republic gradually blurred into the idea of America as the chief steward of a new global order.

No single nation could be trusted with its own fate.

Across the Atlantic, the same evolution unfolded with its own cadence. The early institutions that would one day become the European Union were staffed by men whose war-weary realism had calcified into a doctrine. No single nation could be trusted with its own fate. Europe must bind itself together, not through sentiment but through systems—trade unions, agricultural policies, coal-and-steel boards, and tariff harmonizations. Politics became paperwork; paperwork became destiny.

Each step in this direction seemed reasonable, even prudent. But when the pieces were assembled, the result was unmistakable: A managerial elite positioned above nations, not within them.

And once positioned there, they did not step back.

The postwar monetary order was the most transformative and least understood pillar of the managerial world. The Bretton Woods System forged fixed exchange rates and created a hierarchy of obligations that bound nations more tightly than any treaty ever could. At its center stood the IMF and World Bank, institutions whose power lay not in force but in the leverage of necessity.

A country in financial distress quickly discovered that assistance came with strings—and those strings often tugged at domestic policy. Budget cuts, austerity measures, currency devaluations—the remedies prescribed in the name of stability—became instruments through which supranational oversight crept into national decision-making.

Yet even Bretton Woods was only one layer of the structure. Beneath it, older and more enigmatic institutions continued to operate, none more so than the Bank for International Settlements. The BIS, long shielded by diplomatic immunity and protected by the mystique of central banking, became the quiet court where monetary monarchs convened. They met not as representatives of nations, but as custodians of a system whose continuity mattered more than the political turbulence unfolding in their respective capitals.

In those private meetings—in Basel, Paris, Washington—decisions were made that would ripple around the world. Decisions regarding how to respond to gold flows, adjust interest rates, and maintain liquidity in moments of crisis. These were technical matters, but they carried profound political consequences.

A nation could elect a government hostile to austerity, only to find its options constrained by international financial obligations.

A country could seek economic independence, only to be reminded that its currency relied on decisions made elsewhere.

The financial order that emerged from 1944 to 1954 was not necessarily a grand conspiracy. It was a system built by men, many of whom believed they were saving the world from the chaos of the early 20th century.

But like all systems built without democratic oversight, it carried a paradox:

The more it succeeded in creating stability, the less it remained accountable to the people it served.

And slowly, the line blurred between safeguarding the world and managing it. The managerial state did not impose its worldview through edicts. It infused it through culture.

Universities became the training grounds for the new elite. Foundations such as Rockefeller, Ford, and Carnegie invested in social-science programs that encouraged global thinking over national identity. Students graduating from these programs carried into public life a conviction that sovereignty was an outdated notion, a relic incompatible with the interdependent world emerging from the ashes of war.

Journalism followed suit. Newspapers and broadcast networks, often guided by editors who had served in wartime propaganda offices or collaborated with the CIA's cultural initiatives, adopted an internationalist lens that subtly shifted public opinion. The idea that America's role was not simply to govern itself but to manage global stability seeped into the national imagination.

Hollywood lent its own hand, often unknowingly, by crafting narratives that reinforced America's sense of global obligation. Films and television shows portrayed American intervention as noble, American intelligence as precise, and American leadership as indispensable. The myth of benevolent management became woven into the cultural fabric so deeply that questioning it felt almost unpatriotic.

The result was a new kind of consent. Not the active, enthusiastic consent of a citizenry fully aware of the structures governing it, but a passive consent born of familiarity. People trusted the system because it seemed to work, and because the alternative, chaos, seemed unthinkable.

The decade ended with the world believing it had regained its footing. But in truth, the world had simply entered a new stage: A world managed by institutions whose authority flowed from continuity, not the democratic republic we were promised. It came from expertise, not accountability, and from fear of disorder, not from aspiration for freedom. What appeared to the public as peace and progress was, in reality, the product of careful management carried out beyond the reach of democratic scrutiny.

Yet management alone did not explain the durability of this order. As the machinery of the postwar world settled into place, it did not replace the past so much as absorb it. And the people, unaware that sovereignty had begun to slip through their fingers, would not recognize the shift until long after the managers had already taken their seats. To understand how this managed world could endure so seamlessly, one must look beyond the structures and policies to the shadows beneath them, where influence did not end with defeat. And where continuity became the true legacy of the war.

–CHAPTER ELEVEN–

SHADOWS OF CONTINUITY

"History is written by the victors."
WINSTON CHURCHILL

THE DECADE AFTER THE Second World War shimmered with the illusion of rupture, as though 1945 had marked a clean severing of the world before and the world after. Newspapers declared it. Politicians promised it. Civilians prayed it was true. Yet buried beneath the public's relief lay a truth far more complex, one seldom spoken above a whisper even among those who had witnessed its unfolding: The war had not broken the old networks so much as it had lacquered them beneath new language, new institutions, new justifications.

Continuity, not collapse, had shaped the architecture of the postwar world.

Continuity was visible to anyone who cared to interrogate the genealogies of power that threaded from Berlin to Washington, from Basel to Buenos Aires, from the hushed drafting rooms of Foggy Bottom to the discreet conference halls where industrialists and diplomats met behind closed doors. These ecologies of influence had survived catastrophe by adapting to it, reconstituting themselves inside the frameworks of the new order. They moved through foundations, through intelligence bureaus, through multilateral banks, through academic councils whose mission statements spoke in the gentle cadences of cooperation even as their real purpose remained anchored in the logics of strategic preservation.

It was in these quiet continuities that the real story of the postwar decade resided. Not in the headlines about victory, not in the speeches about democracy restored, but in the subtle way the same actors, the same financial tributaries, the same strategic imperatives slid into new institutions and preserved the very hierarchies the war had ostensibly dismantled.

> **By the early 1950s, the architecture beneath the ashes had become the architecture of the modern age.**

If one wished to follow the thread of continuity through the labyrinth of the postwar years, it was impossible to avoid the figure whose influence lay at the convergence point of diplomacy, intelligence, and finance: Allen Welsh Dulles. His presence, so often cloaked in understatement, was felt not in bluster but in the precision of decisions that radiated across continents. Studying the early CIA means examining not just an organization but an inheritance—the inheritance of Dulles's worldview, shaped during his years among European bankers, industrialists, corporate boards, and the old-money legal aristocracy of Wall Street's most elite firm, Sullivan & Cromwell.

Dulles did not need to rebuild a network after the war; his network had survived it. The same clients he once represented—IG Farben affiliates, German industrial cartels, European bankers who had straddled the war with pragmatic ambiguity—emerged from the conflict shaken but intact, eager to integrate themselves into the American-led order and more than willing to align their futures with the men who held influence in Washington.

The beauty—and danger—of the Dulles web was its subtlety. It operated on the assumption that the survival of Western civilization required the survival of the Western economic class. It was a worldview reinforced by John Foster Dulles, where treaties and alliances were drafted not simply to secure borders but to secure continuity. The Dulles brothers did not see themselves as guardians of privilege; they saw themselves as custodians of order in a world that, to their minds, could collapse again if left untethered from its pre-existing structures.

In that sense, continuity was not merely a policy. It was a doctrine.

And the doctrine nested itself inside institutions that would, in time, outlive both brothers.

Nowhere was continuity more brazenly apparent, yet more meticulously hidden, than in the resurrection of German industrial power. The conventional narrative of postwar Germany emphasizes its humiliation, devastation, and moral and political dismemberment. And yet, within a decade, its economic might had returned with astonishing velocity. It was a recovery so swift that contemporaries like author and journalist Adam LeBor, as well as the Bundesarchiv chroniclers, have often remarked that the miracle seemed less like rebirth than reactivation.

The explanation for this speed lay not in postwar genius but in prewar preparation. Many of the men who guided German industry in the 1930s and early 1940s had already begun planning for a future in which the Nazi state would not survive but the industrial networks would. The Red House meeting, detailed in Allied intelligence files, stands not as an anomaly but as a blueprint—a moment when industrialists outlined how to safeguard capital, transfer patents, move families abroad, and secure relationships with foreign banks, particularly in South America and select U.S. financial houses, so that defeat would not spell "annihilation."

These networks did not dissolve when the Reich fell. They burrowed into the reconstruction, aided by American officials who saw a strong Germany as indispensable to the containment of the Soviet Union.

Cartels were broken in name only. In practice, the reorganized companies retained the same families, the same engineers, and often the same capital. The Marshall Plan poured in money, not just to rebuild, but to re-energize the very industrial engines that had once fueled the war. What the public viewed as a miracle was, in truth, the consummation of plans drafted before the war had ended: Continuity masquerading as recovery.

While ministries and parliaments debated their futures in the ruins of the old world, the Bank for International Settlements remained serenely untouched, a financial Switzerland within Switzerland. LeBor's exhaustive work on the BIS reveals a truth that few grasp even today: The bank did not merely survive the war; it endured it in a way that suggested immunity not just from political storms but from history itself.

Its vaults held the gold of nations that no longer existed. Its ledgers contained the transfers of belligerents whose crimes shook the conscience of the world. And yet, when victory came and committees formed to discuss the dismantling of structures tainted by Nazi collaboration, the BIS emerged unscathed. The very architects of the new world, American central bankers, British financial lords, and the Rockefeller orbit, interceded on its behalf, arguing that BIS's role in coordinating global currency stabilization was too essential to sacrifice on the altar of moral clarity.

Thus, what might have been a moment of reckoning became a moment of renewal instead. The BIS entered the postwar decade not weakened but fortified, an institution whose silent authority expanded as the new monetary order took shape. The bank did not simply survive the war. It transcended it.

In Basel, continuity was not a theory. It was a daily practice.

If intelligence networks, industrial cartels, and financial institutions carried continuity across the rupture of war, the legal codification of that continuity occurred through the emergence of supranationalism. This was not conspiratorial rhetoric; it was the explicit belief expressed in memos, minutes, and diplomatic correspondence by men who feared that sovereign nations, left to their passions and electorates, would always drift back toward conflict.

They argued that the solution was to elevate decision-making above the nation.

The United Nations sheltered itself in a framework of immunities more sweeping than any diplomatic precedent in history. Its agencies—UNESCO, WHO, UNICEF—carried mandates that gradually extended into domestic affairs once considered inviolable. The IMF and World Bank institutionalized financial obligations that no parliament could easily overturn. NATO-bound military policy was tied to a multinational consensus. The European Coal and Steel Community, precursor to the EU, placed industrial output under shared oversight.

Each step carried its own justification, but the pattern revealed a simple truth:

Sovereignty was being managed, not preserved.

George Kennan, whose writings still echo through the geopolitical imagination, observed privately that the postwar order required a "disciplined framework" above national passions. He did not say it publicly because the public might have objected. Yet the framework unfolded precisely as he envisioned: A latticework of institutions designed not to replace nations but to contain them. Continuity became law.

Consider Deutsche Gold- und Silberscheideanstalt—Degussa. The name translates, with a neutrality that conceals its wartime function, as the German Gold and Silver Separation Institute. Founded in Frankfurt in 1873 as a precious metals refiner, by 1939, Degussa occupied a specific and documented position within the Reich's machinery of spoliation: It was the primary processor of dental gold extracted from the victims of the concentration camp system.

The Reichsbank transferred this gold to Degussa's Frankfurt facilities, where it was melted, refined, and reintroduced into the German monetary system. Degussa also held a minority stake in Degesch—Deutsche Gesellschaft für Schädlingsbekämpfung—the company that manufactured Zyklon B, the gas used in the extermination chambers at Auschwitz and other death camps. Both relationships were documented in Allied investigative records compiled between 1945 and 1947.

No Degussa executive was prosecuted at Nuremberg. The company was not dissolved by the Allied Control Council. It was subjected to a denazification process that removed several senior officials and left the institution's corporate structure intact. By 1952, Degussa was a publicly traded company on the Frankfurt Stock Exchange.

By the 1960s, it had diversified into specialty chemicals and pharmaceuticals, becoming one of West Germany's significant industrial corporations. It merged with Hüls AG in 1998 to form Degussa-Hüls, then merged again in 2001 with SKW Trostberg to form Degussa AG, and was absorbed into Evonik Industries, a diversified chemicals conglomerate partially owned by the German government's RAG Foundation.

In 1999, a Degussa subsidiary was identified as having provided the anti-graffiti coating for the Holocaust Memorial in Berlin—the same product line descended from Zyklon B's chemical patents. The company withdrew from the project when the connection was reported in the German press.

The building of the memorial was delayed. The company continued. This is what continuity looks like when documented in a single corporate biography. Not ideology preserved, nor pivotal players masked. Just the institution, moving forward, adapting its products and its public identity, carrying within its balance sheet the unexamined capital of the world it had helped make.

Perhaps the most sophisticated aspect of the continuity project was the way it was hidden in plain sight.

Popular culture painted the 1950s as an era of uncomplicated prosperity, domestic serenity, and patriotic unity. Television shows, magazines, and even school textbooks framed the decade as a triumph not only of American victory but of American virtue—the natural outcome of a democratic nation that had earned its place at the helm of global responsibility.

But this narrative obscured as much as it revealed. The stability that the public experienced was real, but it had been engineered.

News stations highlighted the threat of communism abroad while ignoring the consolidation of managerial authority at home. The language of global responsibility gradually supplanted the language of national interest. Expertise became the new priesthood, and the public, unaware of the magnitude of the shift, accepted the quiet transfer of authority as though it were simply the maturation of a victorious nation.

The decade between 1944 and 1954 was...the design phase of the architecture we still inhabit today.

The beauty of the system was that it rarely required coercion. Its success lay in its subtlety, in the way it aligned institutional incentives with public aspirations, in the way it cloaked continuity in the vocabulary of peace.

By the end of the decade, the wartime networks had not dissolved; they had become the pillars of the modern world. And the public, living in comfort, never saw the shadows at its feet.

The decade between 1944 and 1954 is often treated as a period of transition, a bridge between catastrophe and the Cold War. But in truth, it was not a bridge. It was a blueprint—the design phase of the architecture we still inhabit today. The continuity preserved through intelligence networks, industrial alliances, financial institutions, and supranational law became the skeleton of a new global order. What had once operated behind curtains now operated behind acronyms. What had once been the domain of elites became the domain of institutions. What had once been described privately as "management" became publicly described as "cooperation."

This was the genius and the peril of the continuity project. The shadows of the old world were never banished. They simply learned to move differently. Intelligence channels, industrial alliances, and political relationships proved remarkably resilient, carrying forth the priorities of the old beneath the language of the new.

Yet even these shadows required a sustaining force, something capable of moving silently across borders, binding institutions together, and enforcing stability without spectacle. That force was neither ideology nor military might. But rather—it was capital.

–CHAPTER TWELVE–

THE QUIET HAND OF FINANCE

> *"The Federal Reserve definitely caused the Great Depression."*
>
> MILTON FRIEDMAN

IN THE YEARS IMMEDIATELY following the war, diplomats, generals, and politicians dominated the public theater—men whose names filled newspapers and whose speeches stitched together a narrative of triumph and reconstruction. Yet beneath that surface lay another stratum of influence, one that moved with far greater discretion. These were the stewards of capital, the architects of international banking, the custodians of flows that transcended borders. Their influence did not announce itself in declarations. It unfolded in ledgers, corridors, and late-night cables between Basel and Washington, London, and New York.

Finance had always been the invisible companion of diplomacy. Still, after 1944, it evolved into something more potent: An architecture capable of shaping geopolitics not merely by funding governments, but by determining the constraints within which governments could act. Money became not just a resource but a form of governance, an instrument of quiet compulsion in a world that was too exhausted to resist and too frightened to question.

The public believed the war had been won by the armies.

Those who understood the machinery of the new order knew it had been settled by balance sheets.

The men who controlled those balance sheets—central bankers, international financiers, monetary theorists, and the discreet intermediaries who could move capital across oceans with a few coded instructions—possessed something rarer than influence: *Continuity*. They had survived the war, often by threading a careful path between allegiance and pragmatism. And, now, they found they personified indispensability to the reconstruction of a world in need of stability at any cost. But stability, as it turned out, had a price of its own.

The conference at Bretton Woods, held in the summer of 1944 against the postcard scenery of New Hampshire forests, has often been portrayed as an act of visionary idealism—a moment when nations, weary of destruction, joined hands to build a financial order that would prevent future calamity. Yet the deeper one ventures into the transcripts, drafts, and private correspondences of the event, the more Bretton Woods reveals itself not merely as a peace treaty of finance, but as a calculated transfer of authority to institutions designed to operate beyond democratic reach.

The International Monetary Fund and the World Bank would become the most public faces of this new order. But their most important function lay in the underlying doctrine they encoded.

National economies, once sovereign and self-directing, were now to be interdependent components of a global system guided by experts. And those experts understood that stability required discipline—discipline that elected governments could not always be trusted to exercise. Thus, the logic of conditionality was born.

Nations seeking funds would accept surveillance, and in exchange for liquidity, they surrendered a measure of autonomy. It was a subtle transaction, one that the public barely noticed, but it marked a turning point in the philosophy of governance. The primacy of the nation-state was giving way to the primacy of the system.

Bretton Woods was the first draft of the world as we know it. Its authors, though seldom remembered by name, wrote in the language of inevitability.

While official institutions provided the skeletal structure of the new financial order, the muscles and sinews belonged to a constellation of private actors whose influence spanned continents and generations. At the center of these networks stood the Rockefeller interests—an empire of banks, foundations, corporate holdings, and philanthropic ventures that traced their origins to oil but had long since evolved into laboratories of international strategy.

The Rockefellers understood something that many elected officials did not: That finance was not simply a means of exchange, but a tool of orientation. Through their foundations, they funded economic research across universities, nurturing a generation of scholars who thought in terms of systems, not borders. They supported international development programs that extended American influence into regions where diplomats rarely ventured. They backed institutions—some public, some private, some existing in the gray zone between. This would later become indispensable to the global machinery of governance.

But the most striking aspect of the Rockefeller imprint was its subtlety. There was no single decree and no overt manifesto to define their vision. Instead, their influence lived in the diffusion of ideas, in the quiet elevation of experts whose worldview matched their own, in the discreet shaping of economic norms that gradually became unquestioned truths.

Where elected governments saw short-term political cycles, the Rockefeller network saw decades.

Where voters saw national interest, the network saw interdependence.

Where politicians argued over budgets, the network drafted the assumptions behind them.

Its influence was like osmosis, a gentle, continuous force that few identified as power.

Even as Washington assumed leadership of the postwar financial order, London retained something far more durable than empire: *Expertise*. The City of London—its bankers, brokers, merchant houses, and discreetly connected firms—was the quiet veteran of centuries of global finance. Though Britain's geopolitical clout had diminished, the City remained a nexus where capital moved fluidly between continents, shielded by the labyrinth of offshore jurisdictions that had once served the colonial apparatus and now serviced a new class of global actors.

These banking channels, fortified by law firms and trust structures, rooted in imperial habit, provided a sanctuary for wealth in transition. This included:

- Remnants of European fortunes fleeing the war
- Industrial holdings repositioned from Germany
- Accumulations of capital that no nation wanted traced too closely

The City's genius was its duality. It appeared deferential to the American-led system while simultaneously preserving a private domain of autonomy—an unspoken pact among financial elites who understood that the world's most consequential deals were best conducted in quiet.

The offshore world, which would later explode into public controversy, began as a project of continuity. It allowed old networks to survive under new names. It allowed capital to flow without political oversight. And it ensured that no matter how the map of nations changed, the map of money would remain intact.

In this respect, London did not lose an empire. It merely changed its geography.

The stunning resurgence of German industry remains one of the great marvels of twentieth-century economic history, astonishing in its speed, its scale, and its apparent defiance of logic. But the closer one examines the postwar reconstruction, the more the miracle reveals itself not as spontaneous regeneration but as the fulfillment of a continuity carefully preserved beneath the rubble.

The federal government in Bonn, staffed in critical departments by bureaucrats whose institutional memories long predated 1945, cooperated closely with industrial leaders whose families had guided German capital through periods of imperial expansion, Weimar collapse, Nazi coordination, and now democratic rebirth. The Marshall Plan provided the infusion. However, the reconstruction plan was already created by the same individuals who had previously occupied positions in the boardrooms of IG Farben, Krupp, and the financial institutions that funded the Reich's rise.

American officials, many of whom had interacted with these industrialists through wartime back-channels or prewar legal representation, saw in them not remnants of a disgraced past but indispensable partners for the Cold War future. They were rehabilitated not because their histories were forgotten, but because their competencies were needed. They offered continuity—an industrial and financial muscle that could stand as a bulwark against Soviet dominion.

Thus, Germany's postwar ascent was less a miracle than a reinstatement—a carefully managed return to influence, sanctified by the imperatives of a world divided.

No institution embodies the quiet hand of finance more fully than the Bank for International Settlements, the austere organism at the heart of Europe whose power lay not in the size of its staff or the grandeur of its building, but in its nature of immunity. The BIS was not bound by national courts. Its archives could not be seized. Its meetings, layered in procedural discretion, hosted the world's central bankers in a sanctuary where the concerns of electorates were mere abstractions.

This was no accident.

The architects of the BIS had designed it to be the one institution incapable of collapse, immune to the political upheavals that shattered empires and toppled regimes. And after the war, when certain Allied officials sought to dismantle it for its ties to wartime German finance, the most prominent defenders of the bank were not Europeans but Americans. These Americans were men whose careers straddled both private finance and public service, men who understood that a world rebuilt on fragile currencies required a neutral spine.

Thus, the BIS did not merely survive wartime controversy. It emerged with renewed authority. From its conference rooms, decisions were made that shaped exchange rates, credit lines, monetary reserves, and stabilization policies of nations whose citizens had never heard its name. It was the perfect expression of the postwar financial creed: Sovereignty subordinated to expertise and politics tempered by the invisible equilibrium of the global system.

If diplomats sketched the outlines of the postwar order, the BIS inked its contours.

The rise of the U.S. dollar as the world's reserve currency is often celebrated as a triumph of American economic strength. Still, in reality, it was also the most powerful instrument of influence ever devised. To peg currencies to the dollar was to tether national fortunes to decisions made in Washington and, indirectly, in the boardrooms and studies where the American financial class shaped the nation's policies.

This arrangement granted the United States extraordinary leverage. It enabled American officials to influence the domestic policies of countries far beyond their borders, to bail out or discipline allies, to guide global trade patterns, and to compel alignment through economic necessity. But it also created a paradox: Nations dependent on the dollar lacked autonomy. America found itself not merely leading the world but responsible for stabilizing it—an obligation that would, over time, strain the very structure it had built.

The dollar system brought prosperity, but it also brought entanglement. And entanglement, once established, was nearly impossible to unwind.

The dollar system brought prosperity, but it also brought entanglement.

The most enduring influence of the postwar financial order did not lie in the institutions themselves but in the minds of the men and women trained to sustain them—universities funded by foundations shaped curricula around international economics, development theory, and systemic thinking. Students were taught that interdependence was not a possibility but an inevitability, that sovereignty was a variable of diminishing relevance, that the world of the future would be too complex for democratic majorities to govern unaided.

These students, many of whom would later become economists, diplomats, think tank analysts, intelligence officers, and corporate strategists, carried with them the unspoken creed of the postwar elite. They believed that expertise justifies authority, that global problems require global oversight, and that the world must be managed rather than merely represented.

By the 1950s, this worldview had become the default setting of the Western professional class.

Once a generation adopts a worldview,
it becomes the lens through which all policy is seen.

By the end of the first postwar decade, the quiet hand of finance had become the architecture of the modern world. No battle had been fought to install it. No election had ratified it. It had grown by necessity, by pragmatism, by the slow accretion of institutions designed to prevent another descent into chaos.

But in its shadow, something new was emerging: A realization that the world had not been rebuilt on the foundations of sovereignty and representation alone. It had been rebuilt on management—on networks that answered to systems rather than citizens, on decisions rendered in conference rooms far from public view, on a logic that elevated stability above transparency.

And the consequences of that logic were only beginning to unfold.

–CHAPTER THIRTEEN–

THE INTELLIGENCE WEB

> *"Deception is a state of mind and the mind of the state."*
> JAMES JESUS ANGLETON

THE GREEK CIVIL WAR is rarely taught in American classrooms. It should be. Between 1946 and 1949, communist insurgents backed by Yugoslavia and the Soviet Union fought the Greek government army in a conflict that killed approximately 150,000 people and displaced hundreds of thousands more. The stakes were unambiguous. If Greece fell to communist forces, Turkey would be exposed, the Eastern Mediterranean would shift, and the entire southern flank of the nascent Western alliance would buckle before NATO had been formally ratified.

In February 1947, Britain informed the Truman administration that it could no longer afford to support the Greek government financially or militarily. The announcement represented the formal passing of imperial responsibility, the moment the United States stepped into a role Britain could no longer sustain and assumed the obligations of global order maintenance that came with it.

Truman's response became doctrine. Addressing a joint session of Congress in March 1947, he declared that the United States would support free peoples resisting subjugation by armed minorities or outside pressures—a commitment so broad in its framing that it functioned less as a specific policy than as a permanent authorization. The Truman

Doctrine did not merely commit American resources to Greece and Turkey. It committed American power, in principle, to any theater where the advance of communism could be framed as a threat to free institutions.

The practical consequences in Greece were immediate and instructive. American military advisors arrived. Funding flowed. The CIA, still in its first year of operation, conducted its earliest significant covert political intervention—channeling money and organizational support to anti-communist political factions, influencing the 1947 elections, and helping shape the political landscape in ways that went well beyond conventional military assistance.

The Greek communists were defeated by 1949. What the victory demonstrated, to those inside the machinery, was something more operationally specific: That a combination of military aid, covert intervention, financial support, and narrative management could determine the outcome of an internal conflict in a sovereign nation without direct American combat involvement.

Greece was the laboratory. Iran and Guatemala would be the production runs. Greece taught the postwar architects that intervention worked. It did not teach them where the intervention ended.

The end of the Second World War marked, in official chronology, a moment of closure. Armies demobilized. Flags were lowered. Treaties were signed. Yet for those entrusted with the hidden tasks of statecraft, the war had not ended so much as changed shape. The theaters of conflict shifted from cities reduced to rubble toward the more ambiguous terrain of alliances, secrets, and influence. The weapons were no longer artillery pieces but coded messages, intercepted transmissions, and the human beings who moved silently between worlds.

What emerged in those early postwar years was not a return to peace but the beginning of an unbroken conflict that would stretch across generations. The war would persist, albeit in a transformed manner.

The war would be:

- A war for *information*
- A war for *perception*
- A war for the *unseen machinery that governed nations* long before they realized they were no longer sovereign

In the corridors of Washington, London, Paris, Bonn, and Rome, the men who had spent the war deciphering the intentions of enemies quickly realized that peace posed a more complex challenge. The ideological certainties of wartime dissolved into a new and amorphous threat—one not bound to a single nation but to an idea. It was used as a model of control that spread like a contagion through shattered societies. Intelligence services, hastily assembled during the fight against fascism, found themselves repurposed almost overnight.

Their mandate, once limited to battlefield necessity, expanded into something far more intricate: The shaping of the postwar world order from behind the scenes, preserving democratic façades while quietly steering outcomes toward stability as they defined it.

The dawn of the Cold War did not create this architecture. It revealed it.

No figure embodies the emergence of the intelligence web more fully than Allen Dulles. His wartime tenure in Bern had been a masterclass in improvisation, including tactics such as:

- Forging back channels with German industrialists even as their factories fueled the Nazi war machine
- Engaging in quiet diplomacy with resistance networks
- Reading the fractured psyche of a collapsing Reich in the reports carried by couriers slipping across borders under new names

In those Swiss shadows, Dulles learned that intelligence was not simply the collection of secrets but the orchestration of possibilities—identifying the men who would matter when regimes fell, building bonds that would endure long after the flags changed.

By 1947, when the United States formalized its intelligence apparatus under the newly created Central Intelligence Agency, Dulles moved into the structure as though he had been preparing for it his entire life. The agency's first years were filled with uncertainty, experimentation, and often frustration. Yet Dulles recognized its potential before most of Washington understood what it had unleashed. He saw the CIA not merely as an instrument of national security but as a lever through which the United States could shape a world order increasingly defined by covert alliances rather than formal treaties.

His vision was not born of ideology but of conviction. To Allen Dulles, his form of democracy was too fragile and too slow for the world that had emerged from the rubble of Europe. If the West did not act decisively, and often invisibly, forces hostile to its existence would fill the vacuum. The CIA became the instrument of this belief: A means of stabilizing nations through manipulation when persuasion failed, of shaping elections when speeches could not sway outcomes, of guiding entire regions toward alignment with the emerging architecture of the West.

The Dulles brothers—Allen at the CIA, John Foster at the State Department—operated with a synchronicity that blurred the boundaries between foreign policy and covert action. Their influence reached into boardrooms, parliamentary chambers, diplomatic receptions, and the living rooms of citizens who never knew their instincts about global affairs were being calibrated by forces they would never meet. The architecture was not accidental. It was crafted, piece by piece, by men who believed that the world must be managed before it destroyed itself again.

One of the most controversial and least understood aspects of the early Cold War intelligence landscape was the systematic incorporation of enemy expertise. Operation Paperclip revealed the moral ambiguity of victory, but it represented only one dimension of a much larger pattern. As the Soviets extended their influence across Eastern Europe, Western intelligence agencies realized that the knowledge held by the defeated Reich—intelligence networks, scientific breakthroughs, psychological experimentation, interrogation expertise—was not merely valuable but strategically indispensable.

Thus began the silent transfer of individuals and systems from the remnants of the Nazi security apparatus into the service of the new Cold War order. Men who had presided over operations of terror were reclassified as specialists. Intelligence units that had once served one of history's darkest regimes were reconstituted to counter the Soviet threat.

The ethical dilemmas were buried beneath the urgency of geopolitical necessity.

West Germany's intelligence service (the BND) was built almost entirely by Reinhard Gehlen, a former Wehrmacht intelligence officer whose organization, the Fremde Heere Ost, had compiled the most extensive analysis of the Soviet Union ever produced under any regime. When the war ended, Gehlen and his top officers did not flee or attempt to disappear into anonymity. They waited, knowing their expertise would be indispensable.

They were correct. American intelligence officers, operating under Dulles's guidance, reactivated Gehlen's network nearly intact, providing resources, protection, and autonomy in exchange for information.

Gehlen was not an exception. He was the template.

Across Europe, men with histories scrubbed clean through the mechanisms of postwar political expedience found themselves integrated into Western intelligence structures. Their knowledge was deemed too important to discard, and their pasts too inconvenient to acknowledge. This absorption created a continuity that few citizens would have tolerated had they known. Yet it fused the old world and the new in ways that made the invisible state nearly impossible to disentangle from the shadows of the past.

Among the most secretive structures born from the intelligence web was the network known as Gladio—a constellation of "stay-behind" units. It was designed to operate behind enemy lines in the event of a Soviet invasion of Western Europe. Publicly, Gladio was framed as a defensive necessity against invasion. But privately, it was utilized to shape political currents within nations that were vulnerable to shifts in ideology.

Supported by NATO, coordinated through MI6 and the CIA, and often intertwined with local intelligence services, Gladio units operated as shadow infrastructures. They were trained in sabotage, gathering intelligence, and cultivating contacts within political parties, unions, and civil society organizations. These units, dispersed across Italy, France, Belgium, the Netherlands, Germany, and beyond, were instructed to maintain secrecy even from their own governments. In many countries, prime ministers learned of their existence only when scandals, decades later, forced revelations.

The significance of Gladio was not only tactical but philosophical. It represented a quiet assertion that the maintenance of the Western order required structures capable of acting beyond democratic oversight. If a nation elected a government deemed too sympathetic to the Soviet bloc, Gladio networks could be activated to "preserve stability." This logic, born from the trauma of war and the fear of Soviet expansion, seeded a precedent that intelligence agencies across the West would replicate: The belief that the defense of the concept of democracy may occasionally require actions outside of democratic norms.

Gladio was not an anomaly. It was the blueprint for the covert scaffolding of the Cold War world.

While the intelligence agencies refined their covert operations, another layer of the web took shape in the domain of corporate power.

Multinational companies—many of which had roots extending into the prewar collaborations between American law firms, European banks, and global industrial empires—developed their own intelligence arms.

These were not trivial operations. They included teams of security experts, former operatives from national intelligence agencies, and networks of informants embedded in ports, trade unions, shipping firms, mines, and foreign ministries.

As globalization accelerated, corporate intelligence merged with national intelligence in ways that blurred the boundaries between public and private. Oil companies provided cover for operatives stationed near strategic pipelines. Telecommunications firms partnered with intelligence agencies to monitor international signals. Aerospace corporations worked hand-in-hand with the military-industrial complex to shape procurement decisions that would define the balance of power in the skies.

These relationships were reciprocal. Corporations gained influence and protection. Intelligence agencies gained plausible deniability and operational reach. Governments gained access to information beyond the capacity of their official resources. And the public gained nothing. They remained unaware that the machinery shaping their economies was increasingly guided by forces whose motivations were not national but systemic.

The intelligence web was becoming not merely an arm of government but a network that enveloped government—a system that transcended the formal boundaries of state.

By the early 1950s, the United States had transformed from a nation traumatized by surprise attacks into the undisputed headquarters of the global intelligence order. The CIA's operations expanded across continents, cultivating allies, subverting adversaries, and shaping the political landscapes of nations whose internal affairs were deemed too consequential to be left to domestic actors alone.

American influence, though expressed in the language of freedom, operated increasingly through channels of secrecy. This was accomplished by alliances that did not require public approval, funds that did not require congressional appropriation, and actions that would never appear on any official ledger.

The United States was no longer simply a republic. It was the command center of a new geopolitical organism.

The intelligence web did more than gather information. It curated reality. It crafted narratives. It shaped the perceptions that guided press coverage, elections, diplomatic decisions, and public debates. It moved through think tanks, academic programs, cultural exchange institutions, foundations, advisory councils, and media organizations funded quietly through cutouts and intermediaries. And in doing so, it shaped not only global politics but the intellectual climate of the postwar world.

The architecture that the public did not see was the invisible infrastructure that allowed the West to project power while maintaining the appearance of restraint. And as this architecture grew, it paved the way for a transformation even deeper than the political shifts of the Cold War.

By 1954, the intelligence web had become self-sustaining, a system governed by its own logic, inhabited by its own cast of specialists, and justified by a perpetual sense of impending crisis. For the men who had built it, the world was too fragile and too interconnected to be left to elected leaders alone. The stakes were too high. The enemies too ruthless. The public is too easily swayed by fear or fatigue.

In their minds, the web was not a betrayal of democracy as they envisioned it, but its shield. Yet the shield had become indistinguishable from control, and the public remained unaware of how thoroughly the parameters of their world had been shaped by decisions made in rooms they would never enter.

The intelligence web did more than gather information. It curated reality.

The intelligence web was not simply a feature of the postwar landscape. It was its circulatory system.

It linked financiers to diplomats, corporations to covert operatives, think tanks to foreign ministries, and military alliances to political movements. It absorbed the remnants of old regimes and embedded them into new ones. It preserved continuity where history publicly proclaimed reformation. It whispered to presidents and shouted at parliaments through orchestrated crises. It defined threats and then offered solutions to the threats it defined.

It is in this web that the modern world was woven—not through conquest, but through infiltration. Not through declarations, but through design. Not through invasion, but through continuity.

–CHAPTER FOURTEEN–

THE INVISIBLE STATE

"There exists a shadowy government with its own Air Force,
its own Navy, its own fundraising mechanism,
and the ability to pursue its own ideas of national interest,
free from all checks and balances."
SENATOR DANIEL K. INOUYE

BY THE MID-1950s, the American republic stood at a strange intersection of triumph and transformation. It possessed unrivaled military power, unprecedented economic capacity, and a cultural self-confidence that radiated from its cities like neon. And yet, beneath the surface of that brilliance lay a new architecture of governance that bore little resemblance to the system described in the Constitution. It was diffuse, resilient, and largely unseen—an administrative organism that had grown quietly within the scaffolding of the old order until it became inseparable from the functioning of the state itself.

This structure had no single headquarters. It did not depend on elections, nor did it fear their outcomes. Its authority flowed from continuity, not consent. Americans would come to call it many things: The "Deep State," the "National Security State," the "Intelligence Establishment," and so on.

But in its earliest form, it was something older and more subtle—a state within the state. It was built not by coup or conspiracy, but by the slow accretion of institutions designed for crisis that refused to relinquish their power once the crisis had passed.

The men who nurtured this shadow system would have recoiled from the suggestion that they were undermining the best interests of the people. In their view, they were safeguarding them. They had seen the consequences of vulnerability, the ease with which a nation could fall to tyranny, and the speed with which chaos could engulf a continent. They believed the American people needed protection not only from foreign enemies, but from the unpredictability of politics itself. The invisible state emerged not because someone plotted against the republic, but because those entrusted with its safety believed the dangers of the age required permanence, where the Constitution had stated malleability in governance by and for the people.

In this tension, between intention and outcome, and vigilance and overreach, the modern American state took on a new form.

Every major component of the invisible state began as a temporary measure. Wartime agencies designed to manage logistics, information, and industrial capacity survived the armistice and expanded their mandates. Intelligence units created to break the codes of the Axis powers reorganized into permanent espionage networks. Advisory committees formed to coordinate scientific research during the war evolved into standing councils that shaped national policy. Emergency authorities invoked to ensure victory became the foundation for a managerial philosophy that outlived the war by decades.

The National Security Act of 1947, often cited as the origin point of the postwar security order, was less a birth certificate than an acknowledgment of transformations already underway. The creation of the National Security Council formalized an advisory body whose influence flowed not from statutory mandate but from its proximity to the president. The establishment of the CIA institutionalized a culture of secrecy that had taken root during wartime intelligence operations. The reorganization of the military into a unified Department of Defense solidified a structure capable of projecting American power across the globe with the efficiency of a multinational corporation.

These changes were justified by the specter of Soviet expansion, and to a degree, they were necessary. But as the Cold War progressed, the apparatus built to counter external threats began to reshape internal governance. Decisions that once belonged to Congress migrated into classified briefings. Foreign policy that once required public debate became the domain of interdepartmental committees. The levers of national power moved farther from the reach of ordinary citizens and closer to the hands of specialists who believed they understood the world's fragility better than those elected to serve it.

The Constitution had not been overturned. It had been outpaced.

Secrecy, in wartime, is a necessity. In peacetime, it becomes a currency.

The invisible state thrived on its ability to act where scrutiny could not reach. Classified budgets funded operations that would have been politically impossible if exposed to daylight. Programs buried within the labyrinth of defense appropriations allowed the intelligence community to cultivate technologies, alliances, and proxy networks beyond the scope of public oversight.

Secrecy, in wartime, is a necessity. In peacetime, it becomes a currency.

The structure of secrecy itself became a kind of invisible ledger—one that recorded obligations not on paper but in relationships. Generals depended on intelligence analysts for threat assessments that justified new weapons systems. Politicians relied on covert operatives to influence foreign governments in ways diplomacy could not. Corporations, especially those within the defense and energy sectors, forged partnerships with intelligence services that gave them access to global markets in exchange for information that would shape geopolitical strategy.

In this environment, knowledge became power in the most literal sense. Control of information led to control of outcomes. Those who controlled access to information controlled those outcomes even more. And gradually, the flow of information became less democratic, more hierarchical, concentrated within a network of institutions whose employees answered not to citizens but to supervisors, clearances, and need-to-knows.

It was in these quiet exchanges—the memoranda, the briefings, and the unspoken understandings—that the invisible state found its true authority. Not through force, but through knowledge withheld.

The Cold War provided the perfect alibi for the invisible state's growth. Its dangers were real, its stakes existential, its uncertainties profound. The Soviet Union possessed nuclear weapons, infiltrated Western institutions, and sponsored revolutions that threatened to unravel alliances carefully stitched together in the aftermath of the war. Faced with this threat, even the most skeptical lawmakers conceded the need for vigilance.

Yet the Cold War did more than justify the invisible state. It *required* it.

The ideological contest between East and West was fought not only in diplomatic halls and military staging grounds but in jungles, deserts, foreign parliaments, newspapers, universities, and even the minds of citizens. Subversion became as critical a weapon as artillery. Influence became as powerful as invasion. The conflict demanded speed, ambiguity, and a capacity for action beyond the cumbersome mechanisms of democratic deliberation.

In this climate, the invisible state emerged as the only entity capable of responding to threats that were themselves invisible. If the Soviets operated through espionage, propaganda, and proxy movements, then America needed a counterforce that could match them point for point. The philosophy of infiltration that had guided Nazi intelligence operations—co-opted first by the Soviets and then by the West—became a global template.

The irony was unmistakable.

In order to defeat an enemy defined by secrecy and control, America built a system that increasingly resembled its adversary's.

The invisible state's most profound transformation came not through ideology but through innovation. As technology reshaped the mechanics of intelligence, it created new possibilities for surveillance, communication, and influence that rendered traditional concepts of sovereignty obsolete.

Computers—once unwieldy novelties—became instruments of analysis capable of interpreting vast streams of data. Satellites redefined the boundaries of observation, allowing the United States to peer into the heart of enemy territory with unprecedented precision. Telecommunications systems expanded the reach of signals intelligence, making global eavesdropping a routine practice. The emerging sciences of psychology and behavioral analysis allowed intelligence agencies to begin exploring not merely what people did, but *why* they did it—shifting covert action from the physical world to the cognitive one.

The infrastructure that emerged from these advancements—networks of bases, signal stations, listening posts, laboratories, and think tanks—created a world where intelligence was no longer an adjunct to governance but its circulatory system. Information flowed through fiber and airwaves, not through ballot boxes. Authority flowed through classified channels, not through legislative debates. And as the infrastructure expanded, the gap between the visible state and the invisible one widened.

Technology did not simply empower the invisible state. It institutionalized it.

By the mid-1950s, the American government still looked like a constitutional republic. Congress convened. Presidents held press conferences. Citizens voted. But beneath the choreography of democratic life, a deeper reality had taken hold. The visible institutions of our republic remained intact. Yet their power had been partially eclipsed by a network of agencies, councils, military commands, and covert partnerships that operated according to a logic distinct from electoral politics.

The invisible state did not seek to overthrow the visible one—at least not yet! It sought to guide it, discreetly, persistently, and with increasing independence.

Decisions made in public were often shaped by assessments delivered in private. Presidential doctrines were informed by intelligence narratives crafted months before policy reached the national stage. Legislative debates were framed by threat analyses generated by entities whose work could never be questioned openly. And the American people, trusting the system built to protect them, rarely realized how thoroughly their world had been curated by committees whose names they would never learn.

This was not the tyranny of old. It was inertia.

Systems built for crisis
found themselves governing in peace.

The invisible state presented itself as a guardian of freedom. Yet, its existence raised profound questions about the meaning of freedom itself. How much secrecy could a republic tolerate before secrecy became governance? How much influence could intelligence agencies exert over foreign nations before the line between protection and intervention disappeared? How could citizens hold institutions accountable when they lacked the information necessary to understand their actions?

These questions did not go unanswered. They went unasked.

The public was reassured with abstractions—national security, containment, deterrence, stability—words that concealed more than they revealed. Politicians pledged oversight. Newspapers offered sanitized narratives. Academic institutions accepted funding from foundations whose ties to intelligence networks were deliberately obscured.

Thus, the invisible state grew not because the public consented, but because the public trusted. They assumed that those entrusted with the republic's safety shared the republic's moral boundaries, that the Constitution remained the north star of those who had sworn to defend it. And that the sacrifices demanded by the Cold War justified the secrecy that now shrouded entire domains of public life.

The tragedy was not that this trust was misplaced. It was that trust itself had become the operating principle of institutions that no longer required transparency to justify their power.

By 1954, the invisible state stood fully formed—an intricate web of intelligence agencies, military alliances, financial institutions, research laboratories, corporate partners, and international organizations. It did not function as a monolith. It did not operate according to a single agenda. It was more subtle, more organic, more pervasive.

It was the logical culmination of everything the postwar years had built:

- A world where crises created structures, and structures created continuity
- A world where secrecy became normal, management became governance, and expertise became authority
- A world where sovereignty was no longer the foundation of the republic but one variable among many in a global system defined by interdependence

It had become a world controlled by those who believed they understood its dangers better than anyone else.

This was the true legacy of the decade we have traced. Not fascism defeated, nor communism contained, nor democracy triumphant—but a new form of governance, stitched together in the shadows, designed for a world the Founders never imagined.

The invisible state did not announce itself with a proclamation. It revealed itself only in hindsight—a structure hiding in plain sight. Its outlines were visible only when one finally stepped back far enough to see the pattern.

–CHAPTER FIFTEEN–

TECHNOLOGY AND THE NEW FRONTIER

"We had the bomb.
That changed everything except our way of thinking."
ALBERT EINSTEIN

TECHNOLOGY HAD ALWAYS trailed history like a shadow—sometimes guiding it, more often reflecting it—but in the decade following the Second World War, the relationship inverted. Machines began to reshape the political world more quickly than the political world could understand the machines. Nothing announced the shift. No president stood at a podium declaring a technological revolution. Instead, the transformation crept forward in laboratories, defense installations, corporate research bureaus, and the new circles of scientists whose wartime achievements had granted them access to the highest levels of government.

It began with a sense of possibility unlike anything the modern world had known. The atomic bomb had rewritten the laws of geopolitics overnight. Radar had rendered invisibility obsolete. Code-breaking had shown that secrets were not eternal, only encrypted. And as these breakthroughs fused with the influx of German scientific expertise through Paperclip and its lesser-known cousins, technology ceased being a domain of curiosity and became a domain of governance.

Washington's political class sensed this shift before they could articulate it. They saw it in the way generals deferred to physicists, how diplomats weighed the words of engineers, how intelligence operatives looked to signal technicians for answers that once came from informants on foreign streets. The machinery of war had produced a machinery of governance, and within that machinery lived a new class of actors who neither sought nor required democratic legitimacy.

They were experts. And experts, the age insisted, were the only ones who could navigate the new frontier.

The belief that technical expertise was key to understanding the future had a profound impact, much like any treaty from that era.

The war had created research facilities that operated with a freedom unknown in civilian science. Institutions such as Los Alamos, Oak Ridge, and MIT's Radiation Lab had been built to solve existential problems at an impossible speed. Their administrators learned how to mobilize thousands of minds toward two common objectives:

- How to funnel unlimited resources through channels shielded from bureaucratic interference
- How to create small empires of secrecy where knowledge surpassed the clearance of those tasked with overseeing it

As the Cold War dawned, these wartime laboratories did not dissolve. They expanded.

Los Alamos shifted from weapon to weapon, from fission to fusion, from atmospheric tests to underground simulations. The newly formed RAND Corporation multiplied the reach of Air Force strategy, translating theories of deterrence into mathematical models that justified budgets of unprecedented scale. Bell Labs developed technologies that rendered communication global, instantaneous, and susceptible to interception on a massive scale. IBM, initially a manufacturer of tabulators, transformed into a supplier of machines capable of handling data at a speed that governments had never imagined possible.

Washington did not merely welcome these institutions; it deferred to them. Presidents summoned their scientists as often as they summoned their generals. Congress appropriated funds for laboratories it could not enter, and for programs it could not fully describe. Military officers learned to speak the language of the physicists who had designed the weapons they commanded. Intelligence agencies began to measure the world not by what human eyes observed, but by what their machines could detect.

Technology did not merely inform government; it began to define it.

The old world of espionage—the trench-coated operatives passing messages in alleyways—did not disappear after the war, but it became increasingly peripheral. The future belonged to signals. The NSA, born in secrecy and swaddled in classification from its inception, became the quiet giant of the American intelligence community. The agency's mandate extended far beyond code breaking. It encompassed a new vision of surveillance in which global communications could be intercepted, deciphered, and analyzed with a precision that would have stunned the cryptologists of the previous generation.

Those who controlled the machines controlled the flow of truth itself.

As cables carried messages across oceans, as radio bands filled with transmissions from every continent, as early satellites rose above the atmosphere, the NSA, and its British counterpart GCHQ, positioned themselves at the nexus of a global nervous system. Every diplomatic telegram, every military communiqué, every whispered conversation transmitted through radio waves became potential intelligence.

The world's private discourse became, in effect, a raw material ready for extraction. This was not simply information gathering. It was the construction of a planetary listening post.

And it altered the balance of power within the invisible state. Intelligence no longer depended on human intention. It depended on technological capability. Those who controlled the machines controlled the flow of truth itself.

The technocrats understood this before anyone else.

In the early 1950s, a new intellectual current swept through American research centers: *Cybernetics.* Its pioneers—Norbert Wiener, John von Neumann, and Claude Shannon—saw in the universe a series of feedback loops, systems responding to stimuli in ways that could be measured, predicted, and controlled. Cybernetics did not remain confined to the realm of mathematics and engineering. It seeped into psychology, economics, military planning, and intelligence analysis.

To the cybernetic mind, society was not a mass of individuals but a system that could be steered through calculated interventions. Nations became feedback systems. Governance became an exercise in adjusting inputs to achieve desired outputs. Stability became a technical problem, not a political one.

The implications were transformative. If society could be modeled, it could be *managed.* If it could be managed, it could be *shaped.*

RAND analysts began running simulations that predicted the outcomes of nuclear confrontations with chilling abstraction. The CIA experimented with behavioral science to explore the boundaries of persuasion and resistance. MIT and Harvard psychologists studied how groups formed beliefs, how they surrendered autonomy, and how subtle cues could mold their perceptions. These were not academic curiosities. They became tools of statecraft.

James Burnham had been a Trotskyist. Not a fellow-traveler or a sympathizer—an actual member of the Socialist Workers Party, a close associate of Leon Trotsky during his Mexican exile, and one of the most formidable Marxist theorists writing in English in the late 1930s. He broke with Trotsky in 1940, repudiated the Fourth International, and then did something that the intellectual history of the Cold War has never fully absorbed. He kept the analytical framework he had built as a Marxist and pointed it in the opposite direction.

His 1941 book, *The Managerial Revolution,* argued that capitalism and communism were converging toward a single form: A technocratic managerial state in which power resided not with owners or workers but with the administrators and experts who controlled the machinery of modern organization. The book was a bestseller on both sides of the Atlantic. George Orwell read it, argued with it at length in several essays, and acknowledged that its central insight had influenced the conception of 1984. In Washington, the book landed quite differently. It was viewed as a prescription, rather than a warning.

By 1949, Burnham was consulting for the newly formed CIA through the Office of Policy Coordination, the covert action directorate run by Frank Wisner. His work focused on the primary intellectual dimensions of the Cold War:

- How to counter Soviet ideological influence in European intellectual circles
- How to support non-communist left movements
- How to shape the cultural and academic environment in ways that make Western liberal governance appear as the natural conclusion of rational thought

The Congress for Cultural Freedom, the CIA-funded organization that sponsored literary magazines, concerts, and academic conferences across Europe and Asia, drew directly on Burnham's analysis.

In 1955, he became a founding editor of National Review, the conservative magazine launched by William F. Buckley Jr. His CIA relationship was not disclosed. His column ran for years. Ronald Reagan later awarded him the Presidential Medal of Freedom.

Burnham's trajectory, from Trotsky's circle to Langley to National Review, illustrates something this chapter argues in the abstract. Ideologues did not build the postwar architecture of intellectual influence, but they funded and hence influenced the platforms through which those conclusions reached the public.

That is a more efficient system than propaganda. It is also considerably harder to see. Technology had colonized the human mind.

If there was a single symbol of the technological frontier's triumph over geography, it was the satellite. When the Soviets launched Sputnik in 1957, it created a crisis not merely because the object orbited the Earth, but because it revealed that the Cold War had acquired a vertical dimension. The high frontier—once the province of science fiction—became a battleground for surveillance, communication, and psychological dominance.

American leadership responded with urgency. NASA's creation was a public expression of national pride, but behind it stood a shadow infrastructure of military research and covert collaboration. The Air Force, DARPA, the CIA, and the National Reconnaissance Office formed a partnership that gave rise to reconnaissance satellites capable of photographing missile silos, troop movements, and industrial complexes from hundreds of miles away.

In the high frontier, the United States gained something new: A vantage point above sovereignty.

From orbit, national borders disappeared. Distance vanished. Privacy became an anachronism. The frontier belonged not to nations but to those who controlled the machines.

Technology did not remain the possession of governments. Corporations—often those that had collaborated with the wartime intelligence community—became integral to the new frontier. Lockheed, Boeing, General Electric, IBM, RCA, Westinghouse, AT&T, and dozens of smaller firms entered partnerships with intelligence agencies that blurred the line between public purpose and private profit.

These companies did more than build machines. They built dependencies.

American policymakers found themselves relying on corporate laboratories for weapons design, communication networks, and data processing. Intelligence agencies depended on corporate engineers to maintain systems too complex for government technicians. And corporations, in turn, benefited from contracts that guaranteed influence, protection, and access to markets across the globe.

Technology became the meeting point between the state and the corporation. At that meeting point, a form of governance emerged that transcended both.

The new frontier did not announce itself as a challenge to sovereignty. Yet with every technological advancement, sovereignty receded. The ability of a nation to control its borders weakened when surveillance satellites could observe its interior. The ability to manage its own economy diminished when computers could model and predict global flows of capital. The ability to shape public opinion faded when behavioral research revealed the vulnerabilities of human cognition.

Technology was not neutral. It carried within it a philosophy:

- Expertise overrides consent.
- Systems override individuals.
- The world must be managed because it can be.

This philosophy became the heartbeat of the invisible state.

By the early 1960s, the new frontier had become inseparable from governance itself. Technology was no longer merely a tool of policy. It was the environment in which policy was made. Presidents found themselves guided by the assessments of machines. Legislators relied on simulations they did not understand. Intelligence agencies used computers to generate threat analyses that shaped foreign interventions. Corporations built systems that governments could not operate without.

This was the moment America entered—without proclamation, without awareness—the technological leviathan, a governance structure in which:

- Information, not law, determined authority.
- Expertise, not elections, shaped outcomes.
- The frontier was no longer a place but a condition.

The technological state had no single architect. It was built by thousands of hands, each believing they were protecting the nation from catastrophe, each unaware that together, they were constructing a new kind of sovereignty.

Not the sovereignty of the people. Nor the sovereignty of nations. But the sovereignty of systems.

–CHAPTER SIXTEEN–

GLOBALIZATION: HIGH TIDE

> *"Globalization is not a policy choice—it is a fact."*
>
> BILL CLINTON

BY THE CLOSE OF the first half of the 20th century, a tide was rising that few recognized for what it truly was. It did not resemble the tides described in speeches or policy papers, nor the ones historians later tried to retrofit into the narratives of progress. It was quieter, steadier, more like a force of nature than a decision of statesmen. Globalization, as it would come to be called, did not begin with treaties or summits; it began with something far simpler and far more powerful: *The assumption that the world must be managed as a single system.*

In the years following 1954, this assumption deepened into an article of faith among those who had constructed the invisible state. They believed, with an almost religious conviction, that sovereignty was too parochial for the modern age, that the world had become too interconnected for nations to chart independent courses. Borders, once the defining feature of human civilization, became administrative complications—remnants of an era too small for atomic weapons, global finance, and instantaneous communication. The men who had designed the postwar architecture saw globalization not as an ideology but as an inevitability, the natural endpoint of the systems they had set in motion.

This was the paradox at the heart of the age. Globalization appeared to be the result of progress, when in truth, it was the result of design. Blueprints were drafted in the economic boards of the BIS, the strategic councils of NATO, the conference rooms of the IMF and World Bank, the private dining rooms of foundations, and the intelligence partnerships that wove together the Western world behind closed doors.

The tide was not pushed by nations. It was pulled by networks.

Though crafted in the ashes of war, the Bretton Woods System evolved into far more than a financial arrangement. It was, in retrospect, the first attempt at a global constitution—a framework that bound nations into a shared economic destiny whose terms were negotiated not in parliaments, but in the company of central bankers and economic theorists.

Globalization appeared to be the result of progress, when in truth, it was the result of design.

Its fixed exchange rates, dollar-based settlements, and oversight bodies created a world where economic independence became theoretical while interdependence became mandatory.

But Bretton Woods was only the beginning.

European integration accelerated through the Coal and Steel Community, then the Common Market, then the intricate lattice of agreements that would eventually culminate in the European Union. Global governance shifted from the realm of diplomacy into the realm of administration.

The institutions created during the war—intended to stabilize economies and prevent conflict—began asserting authority that blurred the line between technical coordination and political control.

In each of these institutional chambers, the same assumptions repeated themselves.

Stability required integration.

Integration required oversight.

Oversight required bodies insulated from democratic pressure.

Nations signed on willingly, seduced by funds, reconstruction aid, markets, and the promise of peace. They did not see that every treaty, every credit line, and every joint initiative transferred a thin layer of sovereignty away from the people and toward a network whose power was rarely acknowledged in public. The tide rose one inch at a time—and by the time it reached the doorstep of every government, it was simply accepted as the shape of the modern world.

As institutions built the framework, corporations filled it. The postwar multinational corporation was not merely a business entity. It was an emerging political actor—one capable of exerting influence across borders in ways that nation-states could not. By the mid-1950s, companies like Exxon, General Motors, IBM, and the later giants of electronics and telecommunications had become global powers in their own right. Their supply chains stretched across continents. Their executives negotiated directly with foreign ministries. Their economic footprints rivaled the GDP of entire nations.

These companies did not operate outside the invisible state. They were woven into it.

During the war, corporations like Ford, General Electric, DuPont, Lockheed, and Standard Oil had already learned how to work alongside intelligence agencies, foreign policy planners, and central banks. After the war, those relationships deepened. Multinationals became the private partners of the global managerial class, offering:

- Logistical networks
- Research capabilities
- Political leverage in exchange for access, contracts, and protection

This partnership blurred the lines between public and private power. Corporations were not being regulated. They were being integrated. By the 1960s, the multinational corporation was no longer a company operating in multiple countries. It was an organism operating in a single economic system: *The global system*. And it brought with it a new form of influence, one measured not in votes or treaties, but in capital flows, investments, patents, and technologies that shaped the daily lives of billions.

The tide of globalization rose higher.

While corporations supplied the infrastructure, foundations supplied the worldview. The Rockefeller Foundation, Ford Foundation, Carnegie Endowment, and their growing constellation of affiliated institutions became the intellectual engines of globalization. Their grants shaped university departments, trained diplomats, funded international development programs, and crafted the ideological vocabulary of the age.

The language of "global cooperation," "shared challenges," and "interdependence" did not arise organically. It was cultivated—deliberately—by networks that understood the power of ideas to normalize systems long before those systems were acknowledged. The foundations did not believe themselves to be subverting democracy. They believed they were modernizing it, lifting it into a new era of international awareness.

Yet beneath their benevolent mission lay a fierce conviction that the nation-state was an antiquated structure unable to address modern realities. Their reports, white papers, and conferences proposed solutions that invariably required:

- The expansion of international bodies
- The strengthening of transnational courts
- The harmonization of regulations
- The transfer of policymaking authority to global institutions insulated from voters

This intellectual shift was one of the most consequential developments of the century.

It allowed the invisible state to become respectable. Then admired. Then assumed.

By the end of the 20th century, globalization was not a theory. It was common sense.

If foundations built the philosophical narrative and multinationals built the economic infrastructure, intelligence agencies became the enforcers of the global system. These agencies ensured that nations did not stray from the path that had been laid before them. The CIA, MI6, and the later intelligence services of Western Europe operated with a mandate that extended far beyond national defense. They intervened in elections, protected aligned political parties, cultivated friendly elites, and supported coups when negotiations failed.

Each intervention was framed as a defense of democracy. In reality, they were defenses of globalization.

The overthrow of Mossadegh in Iran, the intervention in Guatemala, and the covert operations in Italy, Greece, Indonesia, and dozens of smaller nations were all designed to keep countries aligned with the Western-led global order. The purpose was to prevent regional shifts that would threaten economic stability or ideological cohesion.

The invisible state had gained something new: The ability to enforce its interests anywhere in the world with a precision that rivaled military power but rarely attracted public scrutiny.

On the morning of October 23, 1956, students gathered in Budapest to demonstrate in solidarity with reformist movements in Poland. By evening, the crowd had grown to hundreds of thousands. Someone toppled the city's monumental statue of Stalin. Secret police opened fire on demonstrators outside the Magyar Radio Building. The Hungarian Revolution had begun.

The revolution spread rapidly beyond Budapest. Soviet troops initially stationed in Hungary were withdrawn as the reformist Prime Minister Imre Nagy negotiated a ceasefire and announced Hungary's withdrawal from the Warsaw Pact. For approximately seventy-two hours, it appeared possible that a Soviet satellite state had successfully broken free of Moscow's orbit through popular uprising.

The CIA had been broadcasting into Hungary for years through Radio Free Europe, explicitly encouraging resistance to Soviet domination and implying, in broadcasts that went beyond their authorized mandate, that Western military assistance would be forthcoming in the event of an uprising. The Hungarians who took to the streets in October 1956 had, in some meaningful sense, been told that the West would come.

The West did not come.

The Eisenhower administration made a rapid and unambiguous calculation. Military intervention in Hungary risked nuclear confrontation with the Soviet Union. On November 4, 1956, Soviet tanks returned to Budapest in force. The revolution was crushed in seventy-two hours of street fighting that killed approximately 2,500 Hungarians. Imre Nagy was arrested that same day. He was secretly tried and finally executed in 1958. Two hundred thousand Hungarians fled the country. Radio Free Europe, which had implied support that was never going to arrive, went quiet.

The Hungarian Revolution revealed something the machinery's architects had not fully confronted. The doctrine of rollback—the idea that communist control of Eastern Europe could be reversed through Western support for internal resistance—was operationally empty. The machinery could destabilize governments in Iran and Guatemala, where Soviet nuclear retaliation was not a factor. It could not liberate Hungary without risking a war that would destroy the system it was built to protect.

This was not hypocrisy, exactly. It was the machinery's internal logic, made visible. The architecture of Western power had been built to manage the Cold War, not to win it in any final sense. Management required limits. Limits meant abandoning people who had been encouraged to believe that the limits did not exist.

The machinery had promised more than it could deliver. It would not be the last time.

Then the tide swelled further.

At the center of globalization stood a currency, the U.S. dollar, which became the linchpin of a global economic system, not through conquest, but through the logic of international finance. Under Bretton Woods, the dollar became the anchor of the world's monetary structure. Even after the system collapsed in 1971, the dollar's dominance only grew. Oil was priced in dollars. International loans were issued in dollars. The IMF, World Bank, and BIS relied on dollar flows to calibrate global markets.

This created what historians would later describe as the "informal American empire."

But informal did not mean weak. It meant invisible.

The dollar became a mechanism for influence, more powerful than any fleet or army. Nations that resisted integration found their currencies battered, their markets destabilized, and their capital fleeing overnight. Nations that aligned with the global system found liquidity, investment, and growth.

The tide had become a current, and the current shaped everything it touched.

By the late 20th century, globalization was no longer merely the expansion of trade or the integration of markets. It was a political, cultural, financial, and technological phenomenon that merged the world into a system governed by institutions, networks, and agreements that no citizen had ever voted for.

- The BIS coordinated central banks.
- The IMF managed national budgets.
- The World Bank shaped development.
- The UN crafted norms.
- The WTO dictated trade.
- Multinationals dictated industrial policy.
- Intelligence agencies enforced compliance.
- Foundations crafted ideology.
- Technology removed borders.

And all of them operated under the assumption that sovereignty was negotiable.

The tide had reached its peak. The world was now global. And the global world was now managed.

There was an irony to the triumph of globalization:

> **The more the world was connected,**
> **the more citizens felt disconnected**
> **from the systems governing their lives.**

Elections changed faces, but not policies. Treaties bound nations regardless of public sentiment. International courts rendered decisions beyond the reach of domestic law. Corporations operated across borders with impunity. Economic crises spread from one continent to another in hours.

For decades, this discontent simmered beneath the surface. Then, as generations passed and crises accumulated, the tide began, very slowly, to turn.

Globalization, at its high tide, appeared unstoppable. In truth, it had reached the limits of its legitimacy.

And the consequences of that realization would drastically alter the century that followed.

—CHAPTER SEVENTEEN—

THE SOVEREIGNTY REAWAKENS

"Sovereignty is not given, it is taken."
KEMAL ATATURK

The preceding chapters are documentary history. They draw on declassified intelligence records, diplomatic correspondence, congressional testimony, corporate archives, and the work of scholars who spent their careers tracing the contours of power that the postwar era preferred to leave untraced. What follows is something different: An argument about what that history means for the present, and what the present demands of those who have read it. The distinction matters because the evidence for what happened between 1944 and 1954 is not in serious dispute among historians who have examined it. The question is what citizens, and their governments, choose to do with that knowledge. That question is not historical. It is ours.

FOR DECADES, THE WORLD had drifted as though carried by a powerful undercurrent, guided by systems that seemed too permanent, too expansive, and too intricately interwoven to ever be challenged. Globalization presented itself not as a choice but as a destiny. Institutions spoke in the language of inevitability; policymakers described integration as progress itself. The tide rose, and most nations, willingly or reluctantly, allowed themselves to be carried along its surface.

Yet history has a way of returning to questions long buried, especially those that cut to the heart of human self-determination. And by the final years of the 20th century, one question began to return like a faint echo at first, then a murmur, then a growing, unmistakable vibration beneath the political ground. It was not shouted. It was remembered.

What does it mean for a people to govern themselves?

In boardrooms and policy forums, the question was dismissed as a relic—a sentimental haunt from an earlier political age. But beyond those circles, far from the polished speeches and optimistic promises of global integration, ordinary citizens began to sense that something essential was slipping away. They could not quite articulate it, but they felt the contours of its absence in a dimming sense of agency, as well as a growing distance between their votes and the decisions that shaped their lives. This also brought a creeping suspicion that the world was being arranged by forces beyond their understanding and beyond their reach.

This intuition was not abstract. It was lived. It was experienced in:

- Vanished industries
- Treaties that were negotiated without public awareness
- Cultural shifts emanating from faraway technocratic centers
- Financial crises that were transmitted across borders in seconds

And slowly, almost imperceptibly, the question that had been dormant since the early Cold War reentered public consciousness. "What if sovereignty had not been protected, and was, in practice, in managed decline?"

What if globalization was not a natural evolution, but the culmination of a silent architecture laid decades earlier? If the systems built between

1944 and 1954 had not simply endured, but expanded into something resembling a parallel form of governance? And what if that system rewarded those architects and managers greatly, at the expense of those it purported to serve?

As these questions gathered momentum, the tide began to shift—not violently, not all at once, but steadily, insistently, as if the deep, submerged memory of self-rule was resurfacing from beneath layers of abstraction and bureaucracy. The world had entered a new era—not of revolt, not yet of reform, but of awakening.

The world had entered a new era...of awakening.

The first cracks did not appear in parliaments or presidential palaces. They appeared in the streets, in protests that at first seemed isolated, then strangely synchronized across nations. Those nations shared no language or culture but did share a common disillusionment: The sense that decisions of enormous consequence were being made in rooms they would never see, by people they would never meet, for reasons they would never learn.

On July 26, 1956, Egyptian President Gamal Abdel Nasser stood before a crowd of thousands in Alexandria and announced the nationalization of the Suez Canal Company—the Anglo-French corporation that had controlled the waterway since 1869. The crowd erupted. In London and Paris, governments reached immediately for the language of crisis. In Washington, Eisenhower reached for the telephone.

Britain and France, operating in coordination with Israel, invaded Egypt in late October 1956. The military operation was competent. The political calculation was catastrophically wrong. Anthony Eden, the British Prime Minister who had conceived the operation partly as a demonstration that Britain remained a great power capable of independent action, had fatally misjudged one variable: The United States.

Eisenhower was furious. Not because he had any particular sympathy for Nasser's nationalization, but because the operation had been conducted without American knowledge or consent. This openly defied the foundational tenet of the postwar architecture—Western military action required American coordination.

It did not. The American response was economic, surgical, and devastating. The Eisenhower administration refused to support a British request for an IMF loan to stabilize the pound, which was hemorrhaging reserves under speculative pressure triggered by the crisis. Without American support, Britain faced a currency collapse within weeks. Eden ordered a ceasefire. The withdrawal was humiliating. Eden resigned in January 1957. The British Empire's pretensions to independent global power died in the Suez Canal.

The Suez Crisis revealed the postwar architecture's true hierarchy with a precision that years of diplomatic protocol had obscured. France, drawing a different lesson, concluded that European nations required a counterweight to American dominance. The Treaty of Rome, signed in March 1957, establishing the European Economic Community, was in part a direct response to the Suez lesson. Individual European nations, operating independently, were subordinate to American financial power in any serious crisis.

The postwar architecture had disciplined its own allies. In doing so, it had demonstrated something the machinery's architects had always believed but never needed to prove quite so publicly. In the world built between 1944 and 1955, sovereignty was conditional.

The condition was American approval.

In Europe, opposition to the Maastricht Treaty, the growing suspicion toward Brussels, and the early rumblings of populist parties hinted at a deeper unease, a feeling that integration had drifted far beyond cooperation and into something that felt uncomfortably like centralized rule. Economists reassured the public. Diplomats scolded them. Foundations published white papers explaining that the world was now "too complex" for nation-states to operate independently. But the assurances no longer soothed. The tone itself—the condescension of expertise masking the erosion of consent—only sharpened the sense of alienation.

The pound sterling's postwar decline was not a single event, but a slow hemorrhage—a decades-long demonstration of how the financial architecture constructed at Bretton Woods enforced alignment as effectively as any military treaty.

Britain had emerged from the war technically victorious and practically bankrupt. After six years of total war, Britain's overseas investments, which had funded its imperial strength, were gone. The nation also incurred debts to its dominions and colonies that it couldn't possibly pay back. As a result, the British economy was forced to depend on American loans. These loans came with terms, set in December 1945, that required Britain to make its currency, sterling, convertible within a year. When convertibility was attempted in July 1947, the resulting capital flight forced suspension within six weeks. The American loan, intended to last several years, was effectively exhausted.

The pattern repeated through the late 1940s and 1950s. Sterling's reserve currency status, the legacy of a global empire that no longer existed, required Britain to maintain exchange rate commitments its underlying economic position could not support. Every crisis, from the Korean War rearmament inflation of 1951 to the Suez debacle of 1956, produced the same dynamic. Sterling is under pressure, reserves are draining, and Washington is deciding whether to provide the support that would determine whether Britain could hold its parity.

This dynamic was structural and a direct consequence of the Bretton Woods system's dollar-centered architecture, about which Keynes had warned at the 1944 negotiations. It would place disproportionate adjustment burdens on deficit countries while insulating the United States from equivalent discipline. The Americans had rejected Keynes's alternative proposal, the bancor, precisely because it would have distributed power more symmetrically. Dollar hegemony served American interests. Bretton Woods institutionalized it.

For Britain, the recurring sterling crises were lessons in the practical meaning of the new order's sovereignty hierarchy. Independent monetary policy required reserves. Reserves required American support. American support required alignment with American priorities. The financial architecture communicated this message without any official ever needing to state it.

Bretton Woods had not necessarily been designed as an instrument of American dominance. But it functioned as one anyway. The architecture did not need to explicitly intend its consequences. It only needed to operate, and the consequences would enforce the new order.

In the United States, the unease manifested differently. It arose not from the loss of national sovereignty to supranational structures. It came from the gradual realization that the constitutional republic designed by its founders was being overshadowed by networks of power far removed from the mechanisms of democratic accountability. Bureaucracies grew opaque. Intelligence agencies expanded their mandates. International agreements constrained domestic policy. And the American people, long taught that their vote was the fulcrum of political power, increasingly suspected that the machinery behind the world no longer answered to them.

Elsewhere (in Asia, Africa, the Middle East, and Latin America), the backlash emerged in fits and starts, shaped by local conditions but united by a common perception. The global architecture that had promised prosperity and development had delivered dependency instead. A dependency on:

- Loans
- Multinational corporations

- Imported cultural norms
- Institutions whose authority superseded national law

The cracks were not yet fractures, but they formed a pattern too coherent to ignore. It was not ideology that began to challenge globalization. It was memory.

Long before parties or movements gave shape to the growing unease, there emerged a rediscovery—sometimes intentional, sometimes accidental—of the political philosophies that had once anchored nations before the rise of the global order. People revisited the prominent ideas that had defined the age of revolutions: Jefferson's sovereignty of the people, de Gaulle's insistence on national dignity, Washington's warnings against the "insidious wiles of foreign influence," and Lincoln's view of governance as the expression of the public will. These ideas were not newly radical. They were foundational. But in the context of a world governed by institutional consensus, they felt subversive again.

In the United States, no figure embodied this resurgence of historical clarity more powerfully than John F. Kennedy—not the mythic version constructed by pop culture, but the man who, during a moment of extraordinary tension, warned the nation of a system of "tight-knit, highly efficient machinery" operating beyond democratic oversight. For years, his warning had been dismissed as Cold War rhetoric. But as the architecture described in earlier chapters became visible through decades of accumulated documentation, Kennedy's words gained new sharpness. They felt less like a metaphor and more like foresight.

His warning joined Washington's farewell address in forming a kind of bookend to American political memory. Two presidents, separated by centuries, described the same perennial danger: The erosion of sovereignty by forces that operate in shadows, beneath the threshold of public awareness, without the mandate of the people.

These rediscovered warnings formed the philosophical backbone of the sovereignty reawakening. They offered a vocabulary for what millions sensed but could not articulate. They provided a moral anchor in a world whose political leaders increasingly deferred to the judgment of global institutions rather than the electorate.

And most importantly, they reminded the public, across continents, cultures, and ideologies, that sovereignty was not a luxury of the past.

It was the prerequisite of freedom.

As the 21st century dawned, something remarkable happened. Nations, long told they were obsolete, reasserted themselves. Not uniformly, not without conflict, but unmistakably. The public began:

- Demanding the return of powers ceded to international bodies
- Questioning trade agreements
- Challenging the authority of technocratic elites
- Insisting that domestic concerns outweigh global imperatives

The outcry was not isolationism. It was a recalibration, a recognition that global systems had expanded far beyond their original mandates.

In Europe, referendums that had once been formalities became battlegrounds. The United States reexamined treaties that previous administrations had accepted as irreversible. Emerging economies began insisting on development models that did not mirror Western prescriptions. And across the world, movements arose that defied simplistic categorization—left-wing, right-wing, centrist, rural, urban—all united by the desire to restore agency to the people.

The invisible state, long accustomed to muted operation, now faced something it had not encountered since its creation: The scrutiny of an informed public. And scrutiny, once begun, cannot be easily contained.

The sovereignty reawakening was not a revolution in the traditional sense. Revolutions erupt suddenly, fueled by outrage and aimed at overturning power. The reawakening was slower, deeper, more reflective. It was the collective realization that the world built between 1944 and 1954—a world constructed for stability in a moment of crisis—had expanded into a system that no longer reflected the will or interests of the people it claimed to serve.

In that sense, the reawakening was not the end of globalization. It was the beginning of its interrogation.

As nations remembered themselves, the world began to remember something older than treaties or markets. They now recalled that:

- Legitimacy flows upward from the governed, not downward from institutions.
- Sovereignty is not a *relic* but a *right.*
- No architecture, however vast or intricate, can endure indefinitely without the consent of those who must live beneath it.

The cracks had now become openings. Light filtered through.

And what that light revealed would shape the chapters that followed. Because an awakening, once begun, always spreads. And in the century ahead, the question will no longer be whether sovereignty can be restored.

The question is whether it will be restored in time.

–CHAPTER EIGHTEEN–

THE RETURN OF THE QUESTION

"When the people fear the government, there is tyranny.
When the government fears the people, there is liberty."
THOMAS JEFFERSON

FOR NEARLY HALF A century, the world moved forward beneath an architecture so vast and so carefully distributed that most citizens never considered it. The institutions built in the decade after World War II—the banks, the treaties, the intelligence alliances, the foundations, and the great supranational bodies that emerged from the shadows of conflict—had woven themselves so thoroughly into a global life that they appeared less like inventions than inevitabilities.

People grew up inside them. Leaders inherited them. Nations conformed to them. And in that continuity, the most important question in political history slipped out of view, buried beneath the rhythms of ordinary life. For decades, it seemed almost impolite to question the system, as if its very articulation might disturb the fragile equilibrium upon which the modern world rested.

Yet no question capable of reshaping nations stays dormant forever.

And this one, perhaps the oldest question in any republic, returned with a clarity sharpened by time: "Who rules?"

It came back gradually at first, more an intuition than an inquiry, surfacing in conversations across continents, whispered at kitchen tables, debated in lecture halls, and hinted at in editorials that tried delicately to name the unease growing among people who sensed that the centers of power were no longer where the civics textbooks claimed they were. The sense of hidden governance, of systems operating beyond democratic reach, was something many felt, but few articulated. It began with local frustrations, with policies that seemed to materialize from nowhere, with regulations drafted in foreign cities, with crises managed by entities no one had elected. But as the years went on, citizens began to recognize a pattern. Decisions that shaped their daily lives were often the product of deliberations far removed from their vote, their courts, their representatives, and even their national borders. And in reality, the people were not benefiting, but the ruling class and their managers were profiting immensely.

The question did not announce itself in rebellion or manifestos. It surfaced as a dawning realization that the civic architecture people thought they lived under was not the architecture guiding their fate. And once noticed, it spread with the force of revelation.

Its return would have startled the postwar architects, those men whose names we encountered in earlier chapters: The bankers in Basel, the diplomats in Washington and London, the industrial strategists in Frankfurt and Düsseldorf, and the intelligence officers who crafted the clandestine arteries of the Cold War. Most of them had not believed themselves to be usurpers. They had believed they were stabilizers. They designed institutions to prevent war, to soften the edges of economic volatility, to coordinate policy across nations whose interdependence had grown too complex for 19th-century notions of sovereignty. Their intentions, however imperfect, were born of a world that had nearly destroyed itself.

But intentions age, systems materialize, and eventually the postwar architecture grew into a structure whose power extended far beyond what most had imagined. A design ostensibly meant to quell the chaos of war had morphed into a structure that shaped global life without ever being understood or ratified by the people it governed.

When the question "Who rules?" returned, it did not simply cast doubt on any one institution. It illuminated an entire historical arc that traced back to the decade we have been unearthing. It was that narrow corridor of years from 1944 to 1954, when the world, desperate for order, had unwittingly accepted systems that would, over time, transcend the very concept of national sovereignty and personal liberty.

As citizens began searching for answers, they found themselves walking deeper into history than most had ever gone, into:

- Archives declassified by attrition
- Memoirs once neglected
- Financial agreements that few journalists had bothered to read
- Records of industrial conferences held in quiet corners of Switzerland and France
- The memos of diplomats whose private views contradicted their public assurances

They found the Red House papers, the Bretton Woods transcripts, the memoranda of Allen and John Foster Dulles, the minutes of early IMF and BIS sessions, and the correspondence of central bankers and industrialists who saw themselves as custodians of a fragile world.

What emerged was not a conspiracy, but something more unsettling: A map of continuity, and an amassing of extraordinary power and wealth for those in control.

The same institutions that had engineered Europe's reconstruction had never relinquished their authority. The same financial bodies that managed postwar stability expanded their purview decade by decade. The same intelligence networks forged against the Axis powers became the invisible scaffolding of the Cold War. The same foundations that shaped early global development evolved into the intellectual engines of international governance. The same industrial alliances that aligned with the West against Soviet influence achieved a level of influence that rivaled the governments they served.

And so the question resurfaced, not because the world sought conflict, but because the quiet equilibrium that had once allowed the postwar order to function had begun to break down. Nations rediscovered their identities. People rediscovered their voices. The centralizing momentum that defined the 20th century met a 21st-century world in which information traveled too widely, too freely, too quickly to sustain the old illusion of benign managerial rule.

On October 4, 1957, a polished aluminum sphere eighty-three centimeters in diameter and weighing 184 pounds was placed into Earth orbit by a Soviet R-7 intercontinental ballistic missile. It transmitted a simple radio beep on frequencies accessible to amateur receivers worldwide. Its name was Sputnik, which is Russian for "traveling companion." Its implications were understood immediately, viscerally, and not entirely accurately by every government and intelligence agency in the Western world.

What Sputnik demonstrated was not that the Soviet Union had achieved strategic superiority, but that it had achieved a symbolic victory of enormous propaganda value at precisely the moment the Western machinery had been insisting that American technological leadership was unchallengeable. The response was immediate. Congress passed the National Defense Education Act in 1958, ARPA was created in February 1958, and NASA was established in July 1958. The defense budget, already large, grew larger.

Sputnik activated something that the postwar architecture had always contained but rarely made explicit. The competitive logic that drove the Cold War's escalatory dynamic was not merely political or military. It was technologically a permanent race in which each advance by one side generated institutional pressure on the other to respond, expand, and accelerate, regardless of whether the strategic calculus required it.

The men who had absorbed German Nazi rocket scientists through Operation Paperclip watched Sputnik's orbit with an irony they could not publicly acknowledge. The Soviet space program's R-7 rocket had been developed partly through the parallel absorption of German rocket expertise—specifically through the work of Helmut Gröttrup and a team of specialists taken to the Soviet Union after the war, serving the same function that the purported Nazi, Wernher von Braun and his colleagues, served at Redstone Arsenal in Alabama.

Both superpowers had inherited the Reich's rocket program and talent. Both were now racing to the stars on their questionable, ideological foundations.

The postwar world's deepest continuities had achieved escape velocity.

The COVID era accelerated this reawakening. Decisions that affected billions were announced not by national parliaments but by international bodies. Policies that shaped daily life flowed not from elected assemblies but from medical, financial, and corporate alliances; social regulations emerged from conferences whose attendees were known to very few outside the global elite. Citizens looked around and realized that the landscape of power was no longer familiar and perhaps had not been familiar or of service to ordinary Americans. In fact, it had been quite constraining for a long time.

The question continued to spread. "Who rules?" And even more importantly, "Who benefits?"

In the heart of Europe, debates erupted over the limits of supranational authority. In the United States, citizens rediscovered the constitutional principles that for decades had been overshadowed by global commitments. In Latin America, Africa, and parts of Asia, leaders questioned the economic orthodoxy imposed by institutions created generations earlier. Across the world, the assumption that nations were subordinate to a global management class began to fray in the face of renewed political self-assertion.

...sovereignty is not a slogan. It is an inheritance...

This awakening was not nationalism in its crude, exclusionary sense. It was something older, quieter, and far more profound: A recognition that sovereignty is not a slogan. It is an inheritance—one that must be claimed by every generation or risk being absorbed into systems that, though efficient, are blind to the dignity of local self-rule, individual liberty, and rights.

The world now confronted a paradox that had always been latent in the postwar architecture. Global cooperation is necessary, but global governance is not destiny. The architects of the 1940s had collapsed these two ideas into one, believing that humanity could only be protected by institutions insulated from the passions of the electorate.

But the electorate had changed as the power structure overstepped its role, triggering humanity's revision to core values. Technology had transformed the relationship between people and power. The old world, built in the smoke of war, no longer fit the aspirations of an awakening world rediscovering its heart and voice.

Thus, we arrive at a turning point in our story, a moment when the long arc that began with Basel and Bretton Woods, with the Red House meeting, with the early CIA, with the rise of multinational foundations, finally bends back toward the question the Founders believed must always anchor a free society.

"Who rules?"

The brilliance of the American experiment—the very idea that inspired revolutions and movements across the centuries—rests on the belief that the governed must never lose the ability to answer that question clearly, confidently, and without hesitation. For decades, the postwar architecture obscured the answer through the momentum of institutions that outlived their usefulness, as they had significantly veered from their stated objectives. But history has a rhythm, freedom has a memory, and the question that returned in our century insists on an answer worthy of a sovereign people.

The story now moves toward that reckoning, toward a time in which America, and the world shaped by its example, must make an important determination: Whether it will remain governed by the quiet managers of an inherited order or by the citizens whose consent they were meant to serve.

And so the question returns not as an indictment, but as an invitation—a call to rediscover the principles that once made nations and people free. And to determine whether those principles still hold the power to shape the world anew.

–CHAPTER NINETEEN–

THE AMERICAN RECKONING

> *"The price of apathy towards public affairs*
> *is to be ruled by evil men."*
> PLATO

RECKONINGS RARELY ANNOUNCE THEMSELVES in thunderclaps. More often, they arrive quietly, the faint recognition that a long-trusted story no longer fits the contours of lived reality. For America, the reckoning that would define the late twentieth and early twenty-first centuries began not with a cataclysm, but with a dawning sense that something essential had slipped out of place. The nation whose founding promise had been the explicit rejection of distant authority and whose Constitution had been written to guard against the concentration of power, now found itself entangled in a world shaped by institutions that neither Jefferson nor Madison could have imagined.

For decades, Americans assumed the postwar order was their creation, a natural extension of their victory. They believed the alliances and agencies, and international frameworks that blossomed after 1945 were instruments of freedom, steadily guiding the world toward peace. And in many ways, they were—at first. But as the Cold War hardened and the global machinery matured, a subtle inversion occurred. The institutions built in America's image began to supersede the nation itself.

By the turn of the century, ordinary citizens sensed it even if they could not articulate it. They watched their economy bend to global markets whose logic they did not control. They saw political decisions constrained by treaties never put to a vote. They witnessed intelligence partnerships operate in shadows deeper than any constitutional framework allowed. Policies that shaped the texture of daily life appeared to originate not from Congress, but from meetings in Basel, Brussels, Davos, or New York, meetings attended by officials whose names rarely appeared on ballots.

This was not a crisis of patriotism. It was a crisis of recognition.

America had not lost its principles. It had misplaced them.

And now, after decades of drift, the reckoning was approaching: A confrontation not with enemies abroad, but with the architecture the nation itself had helped to build. And, with those who strayed too far from our founding principles.

The contradictions were always present but buried beneath illusions of prosperity and security. After the war, American elites embraced global leadership with a near-spiritual fervor, convinced it was the only way to prevent the tragedies of the early twentieth century from repeating themselves. But global leadership quietly evolved into global management, and management evolved into dependence on structures that operated above the reach of domestic oversight.

David Rockefeller kept his most important possession not in a vault but in a card file. Organized by country, then by name, the system cataloged tens of thousands of relationships, including heads of state, central bank governors, intelligence directors, corporate chairmen, and foundation presidents—accumulated across six decades of deliberate cultivation. It was not a social convenience. It was an operational instrument, the physical architecture of a parallel foreign policy conducted from the forty-fifth floor of One Chase Manhattan Plaza.

He had been born into the machinery in 1915, the youngest grandson of the man who had reconfigured Standard Oil and built it again in a hundred different forms. His father's philanthropic empire, the Rockefeller Foundation, the General Education Board, the various councils and institutes whose names filled the footnotes of postwar history, had given him his influence of not only *money*, which he had in surplus, but *method*.

The method was patient, institutional, and invisible by design. You did not need to seize influence. You cultivated, shaped, and endowed it.

You funded the department that trained the diplomat. You chaired the council that briefed the cabinet.

You sat on the board of the bank that advised the treasury. And when the policy emerged, it carried no fingerprints.

Rockefeller earned a doctorate in economics at Chicago in 1940, served as an intelligence officer in North Africa and France, and joined Chase National Bank in 1946. By 1969, he ran Chase Manhattan. In the years between, no private American citizen traveled more widely, met more heads of government, or maintained more direct access to the machinery of global finance.

He flew to Beijing before Nixon. He met with Castro when no American official could. He corresponded with the Shah, the Saudi royals, and the West German chancellors as a matter of routine. His passport recorded destinations that American foreign policy had not yet authorized.

The Council on Foreign Relations, which Rockefeller chaired from 1970 to 1985, was the forum where the foreign policy establishment's shared assumptions were translated into the vocabulary of successive administrations. The Trilateral Commission, which he founded with Zbigniew Brzezinski in 1973, extended that function across the Atlantic and Pacific, drawing together the governing elites of North America, Western Europe, and Japan to align their frameworks before their governments formalized them into policy. Neither institution was secret.

Rockefeller never hid what he was doing. He believed, with the serene conviction of a man who had never needed to justify his authority, that the world's problems required management by those with the expertise, the relationships, and the institutional reach to address them. Democracy, as they saw it, was insufficient for complexity. The Trilateral Commission was the solution.

What he overlooked or ignored was the premise embedded in that solution: That a structure, designed by the world's most powerful private actors, would serve their interests above the interests it claimed to represent. The Commission's prescriptions, financial liberalization, capital mobility, and the removal of barriers to multinational activity were presented as the conclusions of dispassionate analysis. They were also the operating conditions under which Chase Manhattan Bank and its stakeholders thrived.

He died in 2017 at 101, the last survivor of the generation that had built the postwar order from its foundations. The institutions he had tended, the BIS coordination mechanisms, the IMF lending frameworks, the Council on Foreign Relations, the Trilateral Commission, had by then become so woven into the assumptions of global governance that questioning their authority felt, to most policymakers, like questioning the furniture.

That was the achievement, and the problem. Not power *taken*. But power *made* to feel like the natural order of things, which greatly benefited those at the top.

Only in retrospect could the public see what had happened.

The government they recognized remained intact, but a parallel authority—legal, financial, bureaucratic, and international—had risen beside it, claiming jurisdiction over domains once guarded by the Constitution.

This was the contradiction at the heart of the American reckoning: How could a republic built on self-government coexist with a world governed by structures it did not fully control?

The reckoning truly began when the American people—long patient, long trusting, long generous with the benefit of the doubt—rediscovered the memory their founders had left for moments such as these. It surfaced first in disparate voices, often dismissed as fringe, naïve, or crazy. Constitutional scholars invoking Washington's Farewell Address, journalists tracing the genealogy of the postwar institutions, and citizens questioning why decisions taken at global summits shaped their local communities.

But as the twenty-first century unfolded, these voices multiplied.

The rhythms of sovereignty reasserted themselves. The American people remembered central truths, that:

- Liberty without accountability is an illusion.
- Institutions without transparency drift toward self-preservation.
- Sovereignty is not a given but a responsibility.

They remembered that Washington had warned against "the insidious wiles of foreign influence" not because he feared the world, but because he understood that republics must remain rooted in the consent of their own citizens. And, it must serve the citizens, not its elite.

They remembered that Jefferson insisted on the primacy of local authority because he knew the dangers of distant governance.

They remembered that the Constitution was designed not only to empower government but, most importantly, to limit it.

With this memory came clarity. With clarity came resolve.

And with resolve came the willingness to ask the question that had gone unspoken for far too long:

What had become of the American covenant—the covenant that vowed government would remain accountable to the people, and the people alone?

To confront a system as vast as the postwar architecture required more than political will. It required historical understanding, a recognition that the institutions shaping the twenty-first century had been constructed in a different world, under different assumptions, in the shadow of a war whose scars shaped every decision by people who greatly benefited from those systems.

The American people are just beginning to see the architecture for what it is: An outdated, tyrannical, unaccountable, and oppressive force not suited for freedom.

The IMF, the BIS, the UN's expanding agencies, the intelligence alliances, the multinational foundations—all had arisen in a moment of global crisis, when urgency justified extraordinary measures. But urgency had hardened into permanence, and permanence had evolved into dominion.

Reckonings are the province of the people, not the powerful.

This reckoning demands that Americans confront this evolution with honesty rather than nostalgia. The world has changed. The threats have changed. The technology has changed. The concentrations of data, capital, and information have created new forms of influence unimagined by mid-century diplomats.

To preserve sovereignty and individual liberty in this new world requires redefinition, open discussion, and a reform and abolishment of a global architecture that has all but extinguished our founding principles.

Only then can America reclaim its role not as a manager of the world, but as a steward of the freedom that has inspired it.

Reckonings are the province of the people, not the powerful.

And when Americans begin to question the quiet encroachments on their sovereignty, they will discover something extraordinary: Across continents, other nations are undergoing the same awakening.

In Europe, citizens must question the distance between Brussels and their ballots.

In Asia, nations must demand a greater say in economic decisions once dictated by global lenders.

In Africa and Latin America, communities must insist that development must serve local needs rather than international frameworks.

It is not a rebellion. It will be a renewal.

A global reassertion of dignity, driven by an instinct as old as humanity: The desire to shape one's own destiny.

For America, this movement strikes a deeper chord because it aligns perfectly with the creed inscribed into its founding documents. The American reckoning is not merely national; it is a philosophical return to the principle that legitimacy flows upward from the people, not downward from institutions.

The world is shifting. The architecture is revealed. The managers are losing their invisibility.

The American people, long accustomed to believing their nation is immune to the forces that shaped the rest of the world, now find themselves at the center of a global transformation, one that demands they rediscover not only their rights, but their responsibilities.

Every reckoning leads to a threshold, a moment when a nation must choose whether to reclaim the principles it has forgotten or to surrender to the inertia of the structures that have replaced them.

America now stands at that threshold.

The generation inheriting the twenty-first century is not defined by cynicism, but hopefully, by clarity. They must understand that systems without accountability cannot endure without dire consequences. They must see that global interconnectedness is not inherently incompatible with sovereignty, so long as sovereignty remains the foundation rather than the casualty. They need to recognize that the covenant of the republic—the covenant forged in 1776 and reaffirmed in every generation thereafter—cannot survive unless it is consciously guarded.

The reckoning, then, is not the beginning of decline. It is the beginning of restoration. A rediscovery of the principles that have made the United States the great exception in human history. A recognition that freedom requires vigilance. An understanding that the world America helped build could be rebalanced, not abandoned. A realization that the nation's greatest strength is not its institutions, but its people.

The question raised in the previous chapter ("Who rules?") now demands an answer. And the answer, long buried beneath layers of postwar machinery, must return with unmistakable clarity.

In our republic designed by our Founders, the people rule. Not committees, not agencies, not international bodies, not elites—the people.

Always the people.

–CHAPTER TWENTY–

THE COVENANT RESTORED

> *"Guard with jealous attention the public liberty. Suspect everyone who approaches that jewel."*
>
> PATRICK HENRY

THERE ARE MOMENTS IN a nation's life when its people must return to origins, not out of nostalgia, but out of necessity—moments when the present becomes so entangled in complexity, so overwhelmed by contradictions, that only a journey back to first principles can illuminate a path forward. For the United States, the rediscovery of its covenant began not with triumph or catastrophe, but with the quiet recognition that something sacred had drifted beyond reach.

Across the twentieth century, the rhythm of American life had been shaped by forces that seemed as natural as gravity: Expanding alliances, proliferating institutions, global commitments, financial systems that grew increasingly abstract, intelligence networks that blurred the line between foreign and domestic, and technological revolutions that redefined privacy, autonomy, and the very meaning of citizenship. These forces were mostly born from stated noble intentions.

Yet intentions are only one part of a nation's trajectory; the structures they produce often outlive the crises that motivate them.

Americans are beginning to sense that the world they envisioned has eclipsed the values that formed it. Decisions once rooted in local judgment were calibrated to international frameworks. Policies that shaped domestic life were drafted in distant rooms under the logic of treaties few had read. Sovereignty, once the core pillar of the American experiment, felt increasingly conditional—not abolished, not erased, but negotiated in ways the Founders had warned against with prophetic clarity.

And so, a quiet rediscovery begins.

It emerged first among scholars poring over the Federalist Papers, then among journalists tracing the genealogy of postwar institutions, then among citizens who simply felt the distance between themselves and the world that claimed to represent them. This rediscovery is not ideological; it is a renewal of our constitutional foundation.

It is a realization that a republic cannot function if its citizens do not understand the architecture surrounding it. It is the understanding that a covenant, once obscured, must be reclaimed deliberately—with honesty, discipline, and courage.

The Founders had envisioned such a moment.

Washington warned against the seductions of entanglements that would bind future generations to obligations they had no voice in shaping. Madison cautioned that liberty could be lost not only through tyranny, but through gradual encroachments masked as necessities. Jefferson insisted that the people must remain the ultimate guardians of their own freedom. And Lincoln, confronting division on a scale unimaginable to his predecessors, reaffirmed that a government "of the people, by the people, for the people" must never be surrendered to abstraction.

It was a promise. And now that promise demands renewal.

The covenant was never a relic. It was a promise. And now that promise demands renewal.

A restoration of national purpose requires more than patriotic sentiment. It demands clarity, along with a readiness to face the hidden structures, to examine them openly and without defense, and to address them accordingly.

The decades following World War II created a labyrinth of institutions whose influence was pervasive yet rarely examined. The United Nations and its constellation of agencies, endowed with immunities that placed them beyond the reach of national law, had expanded far beyond their founding mandates. The Bank for International Settlements, survivor of every geopolitical order since the 1930s, totally immune and covert, quietly coordinated the monetary decisions of nations without ever submitting to their electorates. Intelligence partnerships, born of wartime necessity, matured into a transnational architecture that operated with a punity entirely distinct from oversight. Foundations and NGOs wielded endowments larger than many government budgets, shaped policies, cultural narratives, and educational programs across borders.

These entities were continuities of power and globalist ideals. They were an orchestrated framework that used expertise as a lever to triumph over national will in order to craft a system of control and stability.

The postwar order had been built, its architects insisted, to make the world safe for democracy.

But in reality, it served the architects themselves.

What will make the world safe again is the exposure and dismantling of the architects of global control.

The new world order must not be ignored.

The modern world was built quietly and carefully by globalist-minded elites who believed that governance by an intellectual super-class and world bankers was preferable to national oversight by its people. This is *Infiltration Instead of Invasion.*

–EPILOGUE–

THE DECADE THAT WOULD NOT DIE

"Everything can be restored. If one won't believe that, how does one endure all this?"

CHRIS CLEAVE

THE RHINE STILL MOVES through Basel with ancient patience. The bridges still stand. The spired medieval rooftops still rise above the Centralbahnplatz. The building near the train station bears no grand columns, no proclamation of power. A traveler passing through today might mistake it for an insurance office or a municipal archive. Nothing about it announces the enormity of what it has always held inside.

You know differently now.

You know what Thomas McKittrick signed in those third-floor offices while Europe burned. You know the gold that moved through those vaults—gold that came through looted central banks, gold that came from the victims of the regime itself—and you know that McKittrick never asked where it came from, because the question, in his view, was not his to ask. You know that when Allied investigators completed their report recommending the BIS be dissolved, the recommendation was shelved.

You know who shelved it, and why.

Ask yourself what kind of institution survives a world war with its accounts intact and its charter untouched. Then you'll understand the Maison Rouge.

You know that on August 10, 1944—while Allied armies were fighting their way across France—men in business suits entered a hotel in Strasbourg through the side entrance and sat beneath painted ceilings to discuss not ideology but continuity. You know what the SS liaison said when he opened that meeting: that Germany must prepare for defeat. You know what the industrialists heard: that German industry must not lose the peace.

You know that Friedrich Flick left Landsberg Prison in 1951 carrying a briefcase, that John McCloy signed his commutation citing poor health, and that within four years Flick was the wealthiest private individual in West Germany. His estate passed to his heirs. He paid nothing.

You know about Allen Dulles in Bern—the Herrengasse villa, the cultivated contacts, the early conviction that the world was too dangerous for transparency and too complex for the consent of ordinary people. You know how that conviction became a culture, how that culture became an agency, how that agency became a permanent architecture of covert action operating beneath the threshold of democratic oversight. You know about Iran in 1953, the documents McKittrick would have recognized as purely transactional.

You know about Guatemala in 1954, where a democratically elected government was dismantled, not because it threatened freedom, but because it threatened a fruit company's land holdings. You know what was decided before the elected governments were told. You know the distance between what was announced and what was done.

You know about the foundations—Rockefeller, Ford, Carnegie—and how philanthropy and policy were woven into a single fabric, funding the think tanks that trained the administrators who staffed the institutions that shaped the frameworks no parliament had debated. You know about the United Nations immunities, and what it means when an institution places itself beyond the reach of the nations whose citizens fund it.

You know about Operation Paperclip, and what it means to import not just expertise but the assumptions of hierarchy, secrecy, and the subordination of democratic will to technical necessity embedded in that expertise.

The postwar order had been built, its architects insisted, to make the world safe for self-determination. What made the world safe was stated to be the need for the continuation of the architecture.

This is the moment the book promised you at the beginning.

The introduction told you that the history of a nation is rarely written in the places we expect it—not in the chambers of Congress or the archives where parchment ages in climate-controlled silence, but in the corners least illuminated, in rooms where the minutes are never taken, in conversations between men who possess no mandate from the public yet act with authority greater than any election could bestow. You were told that what happened in the decade from 1944 to 1954 was nothing less than a reconstruction of the modern world, quietly and meticulously undertaken by men who understood that the most consequential revolutions are the ones conducted in silence.

You have now walked through every room.

- Basel and the BIS
- Strasbourg and the Maison Rouge
- Bern and the Herrengasse villa
- The National Security Act and the CIA it produced
- The Marshall Plan and the administrative architecture embedded within it
- Operation Paperclip and the assumptions it imported, alongside the expertise

- The Rockefeller and Ford foundations and the intellectual landscape they quietly cultivated
- The United Nations and its expanding immunities
- The Five Eyes and the intelligence alliances that outlasted every administration

Each of these, taken alone, could be explained as a crisis response, a strategic necessity, a reasonable compromise under impossible circumstances. And that is precisely how each of them was presented at the time. The BIS was a financial clearing mechanism. Paperclip was a scientific recruitment program. The foundations were philanthropic. The UN was a peace project. The CIA was an intelligence-gathering body. The covert operations were defensive. Each chapter of the story arrived wearing the language of necessity and the face of protection.

What you understand now—what you could not have fully understood on the first page—is that these were not separate decisions made by separate men in response to separate crises. They were streams flowing into a single river. The interlocking pieces of what this book calls the Velvet Empire: A structure of power that expanded its reach not through conquest but through interdependence, through the slow accumulation of agreements that no single generation authorized and no single generation can easily undo.

Its strength was never military. It was architectural. By 1954, the scaffolding had been removed. What remained was a system capable of guiding nations without being elected by them, a system that could endure changes in administration, ideology, and public opinion because its authority did not originate from the public in the first place.

The puzzle that never quite made sense until now is not a conspiracy. It is something more durable than a conspiracy. Conspiracies can be exposed and dismantled. What was built between 1944 and 1954 was an architecture. And architecture, once inhabited, begins to feel like the natural shape of the world.

This is the hardest part to hold in mind because it requires us to understand a form of power that does not announce itself.

By 1954, the work was no longer visible—it existed as a foundation cloaked in process. The urgency that had once justified extraordinary measures had receded into memory, replaced by the language of stability, cooperation, and progress. What remained did not resemble a plan. It resembled an environment. A system not declared but inhabited. A world in which decisions of profound consequence were made in rooms citizens never entered, by institutions citizens never elected, according to frameworks citizens never debated. And none of this felt like usurpation because it did not arrive through force. It arrived through the accumulation of agreements, each one reasonable in isolation, each one building upon the last, until the sum of all of them had quietly redrawn the boundary between the governed and those who govern.

The Cold War gave this arrangement its language and its justification. It simplified a complex world into opposing forces and, in doing so, made the coordination seem not merely reasonable but morally necessary. Within that framework, the institutions that had taken shape in the late 1940s appeared not as instruments of consolidation but as safeguards against disorder.

They were trusted because they appeared indispensable. And necessity, once accepted, rarely invites examination. It invites reliance.

Over time, that reliance produced something more durable than secrecy. It produced invisibility—not the invisibility of concealment, but the invisibility of assumption. The condition in which structures become so deeply embedded in the functioning of the world that they are no longer experienced as structures at all. Agreements made in urgency became permanent arrangements. Authorities granted in crisis became enduring prerogatives. Networks formed to manage conflict became the architecture through which normalcy itself was administered. It became the water in which societies swam, unseen because it was everywhere.

Most citizens sensed none of this. Life improved. Opportunities expanded. Technology advanced with breathtaking speed. America prospered, and with prosperity came a trust that allowed the invisible system to deepen its roots without challenge. The men who had built it were not wrong to believe it was producing results. In many respects, it was. The world avoided another global conflagration. Economies interlocked. Standards of living rose across the Western world in ways that previous generations could not have imagined.

It became the water in which societies swam, unseen because it was everywhere.

But a system that survives not through consent but through inertia eventually confronts a reckoning. And the reckoning, when it comes, asks the question that the system was never designed to answer: Who authorized this? Not who built it, we know who built it now. But who, among the people it claimed to serve, was ever asked?

By the dawn of the new millennium, cracks appeared in the pillars of the postwar order. They did not look like cracks at first. They looked like questions that ordinary citizens in extraordinary numbers began asking with persistence that surprised even those asking them.

Why did unelected bodies shape domestic law? Who benefited from global frameworks that constrained local choice? Why did intelligence alliances operate in opacity, shielded by perpetual claims of necessity? How did central banks acquire such sweeping authority over the economic lives of nations with so little public scrutiny? Why did the institutions built in the name of peace seem to require, as their operating condition, the steady erosion of the sovereignty of the people they claimed to protect?

These questions did not arise from suspicion. They arose from civic instinct—the same instinct that animated Washington's Farewell Address, when he warned against the gradual concentration of power in structures no generation had authorized, and against the insidious influence of those who would promise security in exchange for the slow surrender of self-governance. They arose from the same clarity that drove Jefferson's insistence on the primacy of local authority, Madison's elaborate architecture of constraint against concentrated power, and Lincoln's reaffirmation that a government of the people, by the people, for the people must never be surrendered to abstraction.

The Founders had envisioned this moment. Not this specific configuration of institutions and technologies and financial instruments, but this specific condition: the moment when a republic must look honestly at the distance between what it was designed to be and what it has, through accumulation and inertia, become. They did not design the Constitution to be a relic. They designed it to be a living standard against which each generation measures what it has inherited and what it has allowed to drift.

Kennedy understood this, too. Standing at the Waldorf-Astoria in April 1961, he did not describe only a foreign threat. He described a method—a system that relied on infiltration instead of invasion, on subversion instead of elections, on intimidation instead of free choice, on the tightly knit coordination of military, diplomatic, intelligence, economic, scientific, and political operations. Its preparations were concealed, not published. Its mistakes were buried, not headlined. Its dissenters silenced, not praised.

He named the architecture. He knew what it was because he had inherited it. He understood, with a clarity his successors would not always share, that what had been built to protect the republic was also capable of constraining it and ultimately destroying the idea of individual liberty.

Across the world in the twenty-first century, the sovereignty awakening arrived not as a single movement or a unified ideology but as a convergence of separate reckonings reaching the same conclusion. In Europe, citizens questioned the distance between Brussels and their ballots. In Asia, Africa, and Latin America, nations that had spent decades navigating the conditions attached to postwar financial frameworks began insisting that development must serve local needs rather than the internal logic of institutions designed in and for the North Atlantic world. It was not a rebellion. It was a renewal. A global reassertion of dignity, driven not by ideology but by an instinct as old as civilization: the desire of a people to shape their own destiny.

For America, this movement struck a deeper chord because it aligned with the creed inscribed into its founding documents. The American reckoning was not merely national. It was philosophical—a return to the principle that legitimacy flows upward from the people, not downward from institutions. The covenant that had been bypassed was not broken. It was waiting.

I want to be direct about what I set out to do with this book, and whether I believe we got there.

This book was not written to produce despair, and I mean that. The men who made these decisions were not cartoon villains. Most of them believed they were saving civilization from the chaos that had consumed it twice in a generation. The world that emerged from those catastrophic years was, in many measurable respects, better than the one that preceded it. I can hold that truth and this one simultaneously: that good intentions, institutionalized, can produce outcomes their architects would not have chosen. That is not a paradox. That is history.

This book was written because an informed people are a free people.

That sentence is not a slogan. It is a description of a mechanism. Sovereignty does not require perfect institutions.

It does not require the dismantling of the global architecture. It does not require isolation or nostalgia or the pretense that the world of 1787 can be restored as though the intervening centuries did not occur.

What sovereignty requires is awareness. It requires a clear-eyed, documented, forensic understanding of how the world you inhabit was actually assembled, who assembled it, and in whose interest it was designed to function. And it necessitates understanding where the distance between its stated purpose and its operational reality has grown wide enough to demand examination and change.

For decades, the distance was obscured by complexity. The architecture was too vast, too interlocking, too insulated by classification and institutional momentum, and the simple human tendency to trust what appears to be working. The fog that settled over the postwar world was not entirely manufactured. Much of it was simply the natural consequence of systems operating at a scale and a pace that exceeded the capacity of any citizen, or any elected official, to fully comprehend.

But history tends to reveal itself when the consequences of past decisions can no longer be contained within the language of necessity. The fog does not lift all at once. It lifts the way understanding lifts—gradually, then suddenly, then irreversibly. A document declassified here, a congressional investigation there. A scholar spending twenty years tracing the genealogy of an institution back to a meeting in a hotel room in Strasbourg in August 1944. An investigative journalist following the gold through the BIS vaults. A reader finishing a book, setting it down, and having a newfound clarity of how it all came about.

That moment—that setting down, that finally I see it—is what this book was written to produce. Not outrage. Not fear. Not the paralysis that comes from confronting a system seemingly too large to challenge.

Understanding. The specific, grounded, documented understanding that transforms a citizen from a spectator of forces acting upon them into a person who can name what they see, trace it to its origins, and make informed choices about what to do with that knowledge.

Because systems, once seen clearly, lose their most powerful weapon: the assumption that they are simply the natural shape of the world.

The republic is not lost. It has never been lost.

It has been obscured by complexity, by institutional momentum, by the sediment of seventy years of frameworks laid quietly atop the covenant its founders signed. The covenant does not require rescue. It requires recognition. And recognition is a more powerful act than it appears because it is the precondition for everything that follows.

You cannot reclaim what you cannot see. You cannot reform what you believe is simply the natural order. You cannot hold accountable what you have been taught to regard as inevitable. The first act of sovereignty is not political. It is perceptual. It is the willingness to look at the architecture surrounding you and ask how it got there, who built it, and whether it still serves the people it claims to protect.

The American covenant was never a document alone. It was a compact between a people and their own capacity for self-governance—a compact that required, in every generation, the conscious decision to understand the structures of power well enough to hold them accountable. Washington understood this when he warned that the preservation of liberty required not only valor but vigilance. Jefferson understood it when he insisted that an educated citizenry was not a luxury but the operating condition of a republic. Madison built it into the Constitution's architecture of constraint: Not because he trusted power, but because he understood that power without accountability is power without limit.

The men who built the postwar architecture were not tyrants. They were, in many cases, genuinely gifted administrators who faced genuine catastrophes and responded with the tools available to them. What they lacked, and what the urgency of their moment made it difficult to maintain, was the long view. The understanding that emergency measures, once institutionalized, become the permanent condition. That secrecy, once normalized, becomes the default. That coordination, once established above the level of democratic oversight, develops its own logic, its own interests, its own momentum.

The covenant asks us to hold the long view on their behalf. To see what they could not see, or would not see, or chose not to see. To name what was built, understand how it operates, and make the conscious, deliberate, generational decision to govern ourselves rather than be governed by the residue of crises that ended seventy years ago.

That is not a small ask. It is, in fact, the largest ask a republic can make of its citizens. But it is the "ask" that every great generation in American history has ultimately answered. The generation that signed the Declaration understood that self-governance was not the comfortable choice—it was the necessary one. The generation that fought the Civil War understood that the covenant demanded blood as well as words. The generation that confronted the Great Depression and the Second World War understood that the republic's survival required sacrifice of a kind their grandparents could not have imagined.

Our ask is different. It is not primarily a physical ask. It is an intellectual one. It is the ask to see clearly, to know our own history, to understand the architecture of the world we inhabit, and to make deliberate choices about what to preserve, what to reform, and what to reclaim.

You have walked through that construction now. You have seen the blueprints. You have read the minutes. You have followed the gold and the capital and the scientists and the intelligence networks to their conclusions. The puzzle that seemed like a collection of disconnected anomalies—why did the BIS survive? Why were the scientists absorbed? Why did sovereignty *thin* while the language of freedom *thickened?* All of this has a shape now. It has names and dates and documented mechanisms.

This is what the decade that would not die could not survive: being seen. Not dismantled—seen. Understanding is the precondition, not the conclusion. What you do with this understanding belongs to you, to your generation, to the ongoing project of a republic that has always been, at its core, an argument about whether human beings are capable of governing themselves. The Founders believed they were. Every generation since has had to prove it again under conditions the Founders could not have anticipated.

The architecture surrounds us still. Its institutions persist, its frameworks operate, its assumptions shape the boundaries of what is considered possible in the rooms where consequential decisions are made. But it is no longer invisible. And invisibility was always its most essential defense.

An informed people are a free people.

The decade refused to die because no one, for a very long time, looked directly at it. Now you have. And what has been seen cannot be unseen. The understanding has shifted—not the architecture, but the understanding of it. That belongs to you now. It belongs to every reader who reaches this page, sets the book down, and thinks, *so that is how the world I live in was built.*

The covenant lives wherever free citizens recognize their role in the story of their own nation. It lives in the willingness to ask the questions that the architecture was designed to make seem naïve. It lives in the refusal to mistake complexity for inevitability, or institutional momentum for democratic consent. It lives in the understanding, renewed in every generation, that the republic belongs to the people—not to the networks, not to the institutions, not to the experts, not to the machinery of coordination that has operated, for eighty years, just beneath the threshold of public sight.

The decade that would not die has left us with a choice.

To accept its inertia, or to restore the covenant it obscured.

The choice is ours, as it has always been.

The modern system was not built through invasion.

It was built quietly and carefully through … Infiltration Instead of Invasion.

–ACKNOWLEDGMENTS–

This book exists because others were willing to look before I was. I am deeply grateful to the authors, historians, investigators, and researchers who devoted their lives to examining the historical record and asking questions that were often inconvenient, unpopular, and necessary. Their work preserved the threads of history that made this investigation possible.

I acknowledge Adam LeBor, Annie Jacobsen, David Talbot, Stephen Kinzer, Fletcher Prouty, Antony C. Sutton, Carroll Quigley, G. Edward Griffin, Charlotte Iserbyt, Cleon Skousen, James Perloff, Gary Allen, Dan Smoot, John Stormer, and others whose research into intelligence history, financial power, and geopolitical influence helped illuminate the forces shaping the world during and after World War II.

Equally important were the archival records and declassified documents of the United States government, including materials preserved through the National Archives, congressional investigations, and documents released by the FBI, CIA, State Department, and other agencies. These records help reveal the policies, decisions, and networks that shaped this pivotal decade in American history.

The search for truth is never the work of one person alone. It belongs to all who are willing to ask questions and follow the record where it leads.

My hope is that readers will look again at the past, better understand the forces that shaped it, and remember that truth—once uncovered—belongs to the people. When people are finally able to see clearly, they gain the power to choose what comes next.

–ABOUT THE AUTHOR–

Mel K is a historical investigative writer, media host, documentary producer, and public thinker whose work examines how the modern world was built—not through the events recorded in headlines, but through the intelligence networks, financial architectures, and institutional structures assembled in the decade after World War II.

With a foundation in NYU Journalism and Film and over two decades in Hollywood screenwriting and producing, Mel K brings both narrative craft and investigative discipline to questions that most historians treat in isolation—the BIS and its wartime neutrality, the Gehlen Organization's absorption into American intelligence, the Marshall Plan's second architecture, the Italian election intervention of 1948, the National Security Act's long consequences. She connects these mechanisms into a coherent institutional history of how postwar power was transferred upward, away from democratic visibility, and into structures no electorate authorized.

As host of *The Mel K Show,* she has built a loyal audience through a live daily geopolitical news show and long-form interviews featuring the best global voices and cultural icons. She excels in translating complex political and cultural realities into visual narratives. Mel K's first book, *Americans Anonymous: Restoring Power to the People, One Citizen at a Time,* is a historical perspective and recovery framework offering hope and guidance to citizens seeking a better future.

You may access all the sources referenced in this book, as well as explore additional materials and other relevant subjects, by visiting *www.themelkshow.com*.